UNSTOPPABLE
— THE LIFE OF —
Duncan Page

First published in 2020
by Laneway Press
Abbotsford Convent
St Heliers Street
Abbotsford VIC 3067
www.lanewaypress.com.au
info@lanewaypress.com.au

© Hunter Calder 2020, All rights reserved

The right of Hunter Calder to be identified as the author of this work has been asserted by him in accordance with Copyright Amendment (Moral Rights) Act 2000.

All rights reserved. The author retains moral and legal rights. Apart from any use as permitted under Copyright Act 1968, no part of this publication may be reproduced, scanned, stored in a retrieval system, recorded or transmitted in any form of by any means, electronic, mechanical, photocopying, recording or otherwise, without prior permission of the publisher.

Set in Garamond 11pt.
Layout by Red Bilby Media
www.redbilby.com.au

Cataloguing-in-Publication details are available from the National Library of Australia
www.trove.nla.gov.au

ISBN: 978-0-6450070-0-8 (pb)

Dedicated
to the memory of
Duncan's late wife
Carol Scott-Todd

CONTENTS

Introduction 1
   1. Modest Beginnings 5
   2. Big Red 8
   3. Deadeye Dunc 11
   4. Bound for Vancouver 15
   5. Jackarooing at Moree 19
   6. Overcoming Hurdles 26
   7. Something went 'Wham' 35
   8. Beach Sprints and Surf Boards 44
   9. The Jersey Shore 51
  10. The Eternal City 59
  11. St George Boy 68
  12. Another Door Opens 75
  13. Remember the Alamo 82
  14. 'The Best Year of My Life' 104
  15. The People You Meet 110
  16. South of the Border 123
  17. Stony Motherless 131
  18. The Cold War 137
  19. Konnichiwa Tokyo 148
  20. Ming the Merciless 158
  21. Loose Change 166
  22. Strange Times in Mexico 174
  23. House Hunting 185
  24. A Fool and his Money 193
  25. Hard Boiled 203
Postscript 211
About the Author 213

INTRODUCTION

No one wanted to ride the bloody horse. Speedy Sal was notorious among Modern Pentathlon riders for her unpredictable ways. 'She had just arrived at Fort Sam and she was real green. Hadn't been schooled and didn't know her way around the course. She was just there to make up the numbers.' Those are the words of Duncan Page and spoken with the wisdom of hindsight. But on that hot Texas morning Dunc learned that he had just drawn Speedy Sal as his mount for the coming competition. It wasn't all bad news; as problematic as the flighty mare was, there were compensations for having drawn her. 'Some of the boys decided to toss in a dollar each and the guy who drew her got to claim the jackpot. That was me that day. The memory still brings a smile to my face. That horse could have killed me.'

Duncan knew his chances of a clear ride were zero after he drew the unpredictable mount. He had been warned that Sal would flat out refuse to go through water. Despite the mare's eccentricities Pagey was determined to do what he could to steer her around the cross-country course. At the log jump, Sal balked at the massive mud puddle in front and, instead of charging through the water, attempted to sail over both puddle and jump. She hit the top log of the jump with her front feet and did a spectacular equine somersault. Pagey flew out of the saddle, did a tidy human somersault and landed flat on his back with a substantial thump. A second later, the horse landed beside him with a louder, earth-shaking thump. Lucky she didn't land on top of him. 'That would have been the end of Dunc, mate', he wryly recalls. But it wasn't the end of Pagey, and that's a good thing. Otherwise there would have been one less episode in Australia's sporting history to record. What follows is the story of a unique Australian athlete. The tale of Speedy Sal is but one of the hundreds that make up a lifetime of adventures involving Duncan Page.

UNSTOPPABLE

***

For sportsmen of the current era the idea of committing several years of one's life with no prospect of monetary gain would be considered the height of madness. But a generation or two ago during Duncan Page's era, the lot of Australia's elite athletes was little more than voluntary servitude to state and country. Their blood, sweat and tears were freely given because the desire to represent one's country consumed all other considerations. Australia's history is littered with the enduring names of men and women who pursued their chosen sport for peanuts. Tennis? Hoad, Rosewall, Laver, among countless others. Athletics? Landy, Elliot, Clarke, Cuthbert and the rest. Swimming? Rose, Fraser, the Konrads – and that doesn't begin to scratch the surface. Modern Pentathlon? McMiken, Macken and Page will do for a start. Modern what? Never heard of it. What is it anyway? And who are those blokes?

It's a pity that the three names associated with Modern Pentathlon fail to ignite instant recognition among the panoply of athletes that graced Australia's golden era of sport because Don McMiken, Peter Macken and Duncan Page deserve their country's warm acknowledgement. Like their better-known contemporaries these determined individuals dedicated their early lives to their sporting goals. Like the many unselfish Australian sportsmen and women of their day they sacrificed incomes and the prime years of their lives chasing an athletic dream. Don McMiken, Peter Macken and Duncan Page proudly represented Australia in Modern Pentathlon at many World Championships and Olympics. Their journey was long and arduous, accompanied by onerous trials and moments of great joy. Never mind they only ran fifth in the 1968 Mexico Olympics; that's only part of the story. Their adventures along the way – now that's the *real* story.

How they got there. The sacrifices they made. The variety and number of their achievements – that's the stuff of sporting legend. This story examines their adventures through the eyes of Duncan Page: surfer, athlete, footballer, pentathalete and all-around good bloke. He and his two lifelong companions, Pete and Don, deserve Australia's recognition and warm appreciation.

INTRODUCTION

***

I first ran – quite literally *ran* – into Duncan Page at the bottom of the hill where Short Avenue meets Bundeena Drive sometime late in 1975. I was going for my daily jog having just moved to Bundeena which, at the time, was a quiet little hamlet nestled south of Cronulla on the Hacking River and surrounded by Royal National Park. I'd moved in a couple of weeks earlier and was trying to sort out a jogging track. It was my enduring good luck while on that search to meet up with Dunc who had bought a place on the water a couple of years earlier. We introduced ourselves, shook hands and the without drawing breath Dunc asked, 'What part of the States are you from Hunter?' My Canadian heart sank and then rose in rebellion. What is it about Aussies? Can't they hear when we say 'oot' for 'out'? Don't they recognise the tell-tale 'eh' at the end of every sentence?

Pagey was attired in a ratty old green and gold tracksuit top. I was mightily impressed and asked how he came to earn it. 'Ah well, I was fortunate enough to represent Australia at the Olympics', was the offhand response. That was it. No mention of how many times or in what particular event. My new acquaintance was reluctant to discuss his accomplishments. As our daily jogs extended into months and then became years, he divulged more about his incredible sporting career. Never one to put tickets on himself, the stories were always related in a laconic, almost self-deprecating tone.

If confusing Canadian for American was an inauspicious beginning, it was only a momentary jolt to a friendship that endures to this day. In our years of jogging together and after innumerable trips around New South Wales, I soon understood that I was in the company of a gifted storyteller who was blessed with a photographic memory. These days Pagey falsely claims that he's losing some of his marbles. So, I'm taking it upon myself to record part of Australia's golden era – as seen through the eyes of Dunc and his two pentathlon mates. Given that they spent a considerable amount of time together at Fort Sam outside of San Antonio, Texas, it's not too much of a stretch to describe Peter Macken, Don McMiken and Duncan Page as the 'Three Amigos' of Australian sport. Their genuine and lasting mateship courses through memories of their Olympic years and much of what came before. But before the glory years there was just Duncan Page, the boy from Blakehurst.

1
MODEST BEGINNINGS

It was a balmy Sydney day that Monday, October 29 in the year 1934. A bonnie wee boy was born to Jessie and Clement Page. Duncan McIntyre Page first saw daylight in a small Kogarah hospital just up the road from what is now the St George Hospital. Indeed, it was only fifty yards (the imperial measurement system was the custom of the times). The locality of St George is important to the story because it weaves its way through the long and adventurous life of the baby Duncan.

The McIntyres were that rare breed of early settler who gave active support to the Indigenous people whose land they occupied. Family history remembers the early McIntyres as turning a blind eye whenever 'a bullock or two' went missing. The baby's mother, Jesse Kathleen Haling McIntyre Page, was a descendant of those decent pioneer folk. Readers of Peter Stewart's *Demons at Dusk* – a fine account of the disgraceful Myall Creek massacre – will have noted the name 'McIntyre occurs frequently'. Young Duncan's father, Clement Edward Page, came from further afield – a lot further – having been born in Grays, Essex, in 1900. The union of Clem and Jessie was long and contented and, no doubt, this particular baby – their second (Clement Jnr was the first) – contributed to their enduring happiness.

It was my pleasure to have met this modest and unassuming couple because it gave a clear view of the origins of Duncan Page's remarkable character traits. Between them, Clem and Jessie encompassed much of what made Australia what it is today. The scenario is not uncommon. A gentle and quiet country girl, her feet planted firmly in the soil, meets recently arrived migrant. They fall in love and produce two sons, one of whom becomes an exceptional example of what it means to be an Australian sportsman. Together, Jesse and Clem lived through much of their country's youthful history: the early years of Federation, a depression, two world wars and, after all that, they watched their country become the cosmopolitan nation it is today.

The Australia of Clem and Jessie's early years together was a far different place. People got on with their lives at a much earlier age. Duncan's father, at the tender age of fourteen, said farewell to the grey skies of Grays in Essex and worked his way out to Australia. You heard that right – the young Clem travelled on his Pat Malone halfway around the world at fourteen years old. He hopped off his ship in Sydney and found work for a while on a furniture truck only to learn that the First World War had broken out. Like many young men in that turbulent time, the recent arrival immediately downed tools and returned to the Old Dart. Somehow, he managed to obtain a berth out of Sydney on one of the ships carrying the Light Horse Brigade. The intrepid young man watched while the troop ship passed through the Suez Canal and the First AIF disembarked in Egypt and then made his way home where at fourteen still, he joined His Majesty's Navy as a signalman. So great was Clem Page's proficiency as a signaller (both semaphore and flags), and so high was his shipmate's admiration, that he earned the soubriquet of 'Cy' – shorthand for 'Cyclone'. After the war, Clem returned to Australia on one of two British ships destined for use in the Royal Australian Navy (RAN). The powers that be offered the sailors the opportunity to transfer over to the RAN. The young sailor didn't think twice. Absolutely sure where he wanted to spend his life, he jumped at the offer.

If Cy Page found a home in the Royal Australian Navy, the navy did its bit and found him a wife. A shipmate had a girlfriend, and the girlfriend had a friend. It takes little imagination to work out how it goes from there. Girlfriend's friend and shipmate's friend were soon introduced. Jessie wasn't initially keen on meeting the friend but eventually agreed. The rest is history. Jessie was a dedicated and patient naval wife. Her husband stayed in the service and served with distinction, retiring after World War II as Australia's most decorated sailor (as opposed to commissioned officer).

During one engagement in the First World War off Zeebrugge in Belgium, the Aussies acquitted themselves with such distinction that several Victoria

MODEST BEGINNINGS

Crosses were awarded. There were so many deserving sailors that they ran out of awards and the final two were decided by placing names in a hat. Cy Page lucked out and had to settle for second prize. In recompense he received the Croix de Guerre and Palms in recognition of his valour. When seen together, the vast array of Cy Page's medals is eye-popping. He was never a big man and one could understand how he might walk with a slight stoop when wearing his decorations. To meet Cy Page you would never think that you were in the company of one of Australia's genuine naval heroes – he never mentioned a word. Like his son, he was a genuinely modest and unassuming man. Duncan, who almost never refers to his own accomplishments, is more than happy to speak about his father's. Early morning every April 25th, he lays a wreath at the local memorial and says a respectful prayer. And Jessie, lest we forget her, your son speaks thankfully of the patience and love that most gentle of women showered on him.

2
BIG RED

Cy Page set up his family a small Kogarah house where they lived in the interregnum between the two World Wars. It is worth remembering that Page Snr was often at sea so Jessie had the responsibility of raising two navy brats. Duncan was born while his father was stationed at the naval base on Garden Island and, for those years at least, he was an attentive husband and father. With the outbreak of hostilities in 1939, Cy sailed away with the legendary 'Scrap Iron Flotilla'. The flotilla was to become the stuff of legend. It was made up of five aging destroyers that the Nazi propagandist, Goebbels, derided as 'scrap iron'. Aging or not, the flotilla performed with distinction in numerous engagements throughout the Mediterranean and later in the Far East. By the end of the hostilities, of the five, only two remained afloat and on combat duty. Aboard the flotilla's leader, HMAS Stuart, Cy Page kept the other ships aware of orders with his rapid and accurate signalling. A brief survey of the many adventures that involved the Scrap Iron Flotilla makes astonishing reading. It is further evidence of how in its early years, the Australia Navy was able to do amazing things with a bit of scrap iron and immense determination and ingenuity.

As for his own contribution to the war effort, Dunc remembers standing on his auntie's Kogarah patio with the adults who watched anxiously during the mini-sub attack on Sydney Harbour. No doubt the young lad made Jessie's life a complete joy during those long anxious years. And joy there was a-plenty in that little Kogarah house when Cy returned. There were several more medals on his chest but few words of how he came to earn them. The family patriarch returned from hostilities exhausted and not all that well. But he had come back with an absolute determination to raise his family in a rural environment. The Page family did just that by settling in the peaceful country locale of Blakehurst on the north side of the George's River. At the time it was a place of few houses and many bush blocks. It fitted their needs perfectly.

Today, Blakehurst is an upmarket suburb in the St George Shire replete with brick houses marching in serried rows along winding streets, avenues and closes. The lawns are manicured and fertilised from bags bought at garden centres, not by freely wandering stock. But after the war, the suburb was a different place altogether. Dunc clearly remembers there were just three houses in their immediate vicinity. The rest was empty paddocks. It was a great place to raise kids; and didn't they thrive? Especially the youngest.

One of the Page's neighbours, a chap named Oscar Myers, had an interest in the trotting game. With two horses and a dairy cow on his neighbour's block, the industrious young Duncan was soon helping out with the milking. In return, the boy was allowed to ride Oscar's horses – one an eleven-hand pony with the name 'Tommy'. The other was a trotting mare named 'Ruby'. Pagey didn't have to think too hard when recalling their names and that reflects the hours spent perched on their backs. At that tender age, the young Duncan was learning what hard work could achieve – even if the reward only involved hacking around on horses. Mr Myers's horses and the empty paddock provided the inspiration for a lifelong love affair with the equine species. Tommy and Ruby were the first in a long line. The love of days on horseback with their scent and the smell of leather in his nostrils later took him across some hairy jumps and near misses.

Duncan's industry in milking the Jersey dairy cow quickly earned him greater responsibility with his employer. It transpired that Oscar Myers was also a substantial landlord who owned several houses in Mascot, the suburb adjacent to Sydney's airport. Pagey's job was to accompany his employer on his rounds to collect the rent from the numerous tenants. Mr Myers's preferred mode of transport was to drive a horse and sulky up the Princes Highway from Blakehurst to Mascot. Those who travel that hyper-congested route today might reminisce for that unhurried and placid time. The suburb of Mascot was a stone's throw from Randwick Racecourse and Dunc vividly remembers that most of the houses came equipped with a stable out the back. There was just the slightest chance that one or two of those stables might actually have housed a winner.

Hacking about with Tommy and Ruby was fine for a while but our budding Olympian yearned for a horse of his own. He was eleven years old now and it was time to move on from ponies and trotters. His father agreed and put his hand in his pocket. This is where the employee relationship with Oscar Myers pays off big time. After a few well-placed enquiries, Duncan's employer found a suitable horse, a sixteen-hand chestnut with a prominent blaze – known to his proud new owner as 'Big Red'. Red was a middling handsome horse and seemed a likely mount for an avid young equestrian. The horse's present owner stabled him at Alexandria and, after being allowed a brief test ride, young Duncan had found a new companion. He rode Big Red down the highway to the horse's new home at Bald Face near Blakehurst where he let him loose in the paddock next door.

Modern Pentathlon demands a high degree of equine expertise and the relationship that slowly evolved on the broad back of Big Red provided the young lad with the requisite foundation. It wasn't long before the young rider tired of galloping around the paddocks and felt that he needed something to spice things up. Ever the inventive individual, Dunc built himself a series of jumps by using poles he dredged up from nearby blocks. These were suspended from low-hanging limbs of trees and, in no time, a jumps course had taken shape. Big Red was encouraged to take to the air and the budding jumps rider soon learned to hang on. All this was completely unsupervised and devoid of any adult intervention. How serious injury was avoided is unknown, but the fact is the budding equestrian survived unscathed.

Today's readers may shake their heads in wonder, but things were different then. It is a matter of record that Clem Page had sailed across the world as a fourteen-year-old and Jessie was a country girl for whom proficiency on horseback was a way of life. Worry about their boy on Big Red? How else is he going to learn?

3

DEADEYE DUNC

At the same time, he was developing his equestrian skills, young Dunc was keen to become proficient in another skill essential to Modern Pentathlon – pistol shooting. Duncan's expertise with various types of firearms started early and continued until he became nothing less than a crack shot. In the parlance of the times, he was something of a 'Deadeye Dick'. But wait a minute. A kid allowed access to firearms? A mere stripling of a boy? Again it is important to reflect on the temper of the times. It should be apparent that the Sydney of Pagey's boyhood bears little resemblance to the sprawling, hyper-crowded city it has become in the twenty-first century. Even allowing for the vastly more relaxed attitudes of a bygone era, the vision of a ten-year-old Duncan Page wielding a pistol gives pause for thought. But that was the way of those less cautious days. Although Australia was rapidly outgrowing its rural beginnings, the vestiges of an earlier time remained. In addition to riding into town on horseback or sulky, people thought nothing of carrying firearms, usually rifles, and the firearms were almost always carried in plain view. After all, in an impoverished post-war Australia, who could afford a rifle case? At the time you could wander down George Street and find any one of six gun shops with open doors. Try carrying a weapon on that crowded street today and a SWAT team would come calling in a heartbeat. But in those days the casual carrying of firearms wasn't considered unusual; indeed, it was commonplace – and it certainly wasn't a matter of concern.

Dunc remembers the 'Shooter's Train' that left Central Station promptly at seven am on Saturday mornings to carry passengers to the rifle range near Liverpool. The train service had its origins in the years before World War II and continued long after. In the aftermath of the war, very few people could afford individual transport so travel by train was an essential part of daily life. The shooters heading for the Liverpool range were no exception. According to Dunc, the shooters mostly carried big bore rifles – 303's and the like. The mind boggles to think of carriages carrying heavily armed men out for a day's shoot, but that was unexceptional in those hungry post-war years. People from near and far would arrive at Central Station for a day's outing. Recreational shooting was commonplace and the presence of a rifle on someone's shoulder was hardly headline news.

And did Jessie think about her darling boy's intense love affair with firearms? Not much, it turns out. Remember this, Jessie Page was a country girl born and bred – and country life was plagued by rabbits. By pinging off a rabbit or two country kids would provide food for the family table. It was what children in her family had always done and what all country kids did. Throughout her son's riding and shooting escapades Jessie was never anything other than serene and calm. As much as a mother of two active young boys can hope to be. In fact, she would never have considered her youngest boy's avid interest in riding and shooting as anything remarkable.

Duncan's remarkable and single-minded determination to set himself a goal and then attain it showed up early. His newfound goal as a ten-year-old? He wanted a pistol but lacked the requisite cash. What to do? An uncle living in Kogarah suffered from a bad back and coveted the horsehair mattress on which his young nephew slept. The uncle had a pistol, the nephew had a mattress – the exchange was duly made. The problem with the transaction was that the pistol came with a broken hammer and couldn't fire. Undeterred by that minor defect, the inventive lad set to work with hacksaw and file and soon had his pistol in good working order. Dunc's next foray into the world of shooting came at the hands of his ever-generous father. Cy Page was a teetotaller and not doctrinaire in his abstinence; he just didn't drink the stuff. But that didn't stop him from using it as currency. He traded a bottle of whiskey for a .22 calibre rifle which he then presented to his son. There is some question as to the origins of the bottle of whisky but the grateful son suspects that it may have originated in the naval mess. Wherever it came from, Cy wasn't saying.

Dunc went on to spend many happy hours with his new rifle and Big Red at nearby Baldface (next door to Blakehurst). It wasn't long before he and his horse sought out more distant places to develop his marksmanship. A group of like-minded kids had taken to congregating on Saturday mornings at Kurnell, where they raced their horses and shot up five-gallon kerosene cans. It was a fair sort of ride for Dunc and Big Red. They had to negotiate Tom Ugly's bridge and then ride into the depths of Sutherland Shire. At Kurnell, the serene site of Captain Cook's landing, Saturday mornings resounded with the sound of young men whooping it up shooting at kero tins and generally having a grand old time. Kurnell at the time was largely unpopulated except for the row of Depression-era shacks at Boat Harbour. The kids ran wild learning to ride and shoot and, miraculously, returning home unscathed just in time for dinner.

For the young Duncan Page, all this provided the solid foundation for what was to come later in his long sporting life. The lessons learned on horseback and with firearm in hand at Bald Face and Kurnell were part of the apprenticeship that led to a world stage. It's fair to say that few would have dreamt it at the time, and certainly not the modest young man himself. But if determination and application are prerequisites for later success, Dunc was already well on the way.

***

For a while it seemed that a life on the land was to be Duncan's destiny. His sixth-class teacher, the fearsome 'Basher' Grant, recommended that he and another student be sent to Hurlstone Agricultural College because they seemed suited to the rural lifestyle. There is an irony that the recommendation came from a teacher who, on the surface at least, seemed ill-disposed to the future careers of his pupils. Dunc retains a clear recollection of the time Basher lined up the entire class around the walls of the classroom to receive their due punishment. And the punishment was by any reckoning *in extremis* when considered in light of current educational sensitivities. But in those more rugged days 'six of the best' at the end of an expertly wielded cane kept all but the most recalcitrant students more or less in order. Pagey confessed that he was far from a top class performer in the scholarship league table. He describes himself as 'no great scholar' and confesses to 'not knowing what it was all about'.

With the full consent of Jessie and Cy, Duncan left Kogarah Primary and the tender care of the legendary 'Basher' Grant for Hurlstone Agricultural High School in the far reaches of Sydney's west. The school's curriculum catered for students from all over New South Wales and was designed with the particular intention of preparing them for a productive life on the land. 'Hurlstone Ag' as it is colloquially known has today become a highly sought-after school for Sydney's best and brightest. In Pagey's time things were considerably different – the best and brightest went elsewhere. In his time at Ag school, he attended both as a day student and boarder – much preferring the day school where he went home each day for Mum's cooking and care.

No matter what the curriculum, a long-term formal education was never on the cards for Duncan. As soon as he was legally able, he left Hurlstone Ag on good terms at the tender age of fourteen. Although he describes himself at the time as a 'little fat kid', Pagey was introduced to an interest which became all-consuming. It was at Hurlstone Agricultural College that he took the first steps in his competitive athletic career. On the school's oval, which he describes as little more than 'a cow paddock full of paspalum', the young man developed an interest in hurdling – 'I wasn't any good at it' – and, in time, the event was later to become a matter of distinguished achievement. He persisted at school even though, in his own words: 'I was never the best. Not even good enough to make the footy team.' Despite his self-deprecatory account of his high school athletic career, the 'little fat kid' jogging around the oval at Hurlstone Ag wasn't to know that he was already on the road to the Olympics.

4

BOUND FOR VANCOUVER

From Vancouver to Moree the 'little fat kid' spread his wings in a wide arc. Neither place has much in common with the other, but the link will be revealed in the fullness of time. Never one to let the grass grow under his feet, after saying farewell to Hurlstone Ag, Dunc found work in Davis and Smith's saddlery in Darlinghurst. Not even a lowly apprentice, he was employed to work around the shop where he learned the basics of what would become a long and productive career. Away from his day job, Pagey remained an active horseman and shooter. His interest in the latter provided the impetus for his next great adventure.

A burning desire took hold in the active brain of the saddler's assistant. He was determined to spend his wages on a new rifle. Not just any rifle either. After researching the matter Pagey had his heart set on particular firearm – a Marlin lever action .22 rifle. But where to get it? In post-war Australia, it was difficult to obtain many things and that applied particularly to non-military firearms. Duncan finally located his Marlin .22 at the Hudson's Bay Company's department store located on the corner of Georgia and Granville Streets in the heart of downtown Vancouver, British Columbia. The store's catalogue assured him the weapon was readily available in that venerable institution locals fondly refer to as 'The Bay'. He had to have it. It then became a matter of how to get to Vancouver. Today it's fourteen hours direct flight; in those less hurried times a sea voyage was the only feasible option and it could take upwards of a month.

Time meant little to the now fifteen-year-old and, in his singularly determined mind, the rifle would be his no matter what. Now to figure out how to do it. Step one? Leave the employ of Davis and Smith. He could become a saddler some other time. Step two? Find a way of getting to Vancouver. A young mate he knocked around with in Blakehurst came up with a plan. If

UNSTOPPABLE

Dunc joined the seafarers union, he could get a job as bellboy on a ship bound for Vancouver. His mate, who just happened to be an excellent pianist, also worked as a bellboy aboard the New Zealand owned Aorangi. A Glasgow built ship; it was designed specifically for the Sydney to Vancouver passenger route. The Aorangi was launched in 1924 and was fitted out as a troopship in 1941. It was chartered until 1948, when normal operations resumed. With things back to normal on the venerable old vessel, Duncan Page stepped aboard as its most newly appointed bellboy.

The long voyage to Vancouver – via Auckland, Suva, Honolulu, Victoria, BC and finally Vancouver – offered the young Duncan some valuable life lessons. One of the firsts was how to deliver a martini to a cabin without spilling a drop. The trick, as he describes it now, was to remove the olive and place it in his mouth. Why? Simple. It reduced the level of fluid in the glass and made it easier to transport the drink without spillage. The bellboy would then knock on the cabin door after quickly removing the olive from his mouth and returning it to its rightful gin-soaked place. On the subject of turned stomachs, seasickness was common among the passengers and Dunc was as good as gold after overcoming an early bout of it himself. It wasn't the fault of the olives that seasickness ran rife among his clients. But it had certain benefits. He and his fellow bellboys were happy to be untroubled by passenger demands for dry martinis when the dreaded *mal de mer* ran rampant. A second lesson awaited the intrepid young traveller when he arrived at his destination – when travelling to northern climes in winter it is wise to come suitably attired. This is particularly important when the traveller wishes to ascend one of Vancouver's nearby mountains the day before Christmas.

Grouse Mountain is located just north of the centre of Vancouver. Today it has several quality ski runs accessible by a ski lift and an impressive restaurant accessible by a gondola. In the late forties, the ski lift was the only way to the top. Today, the extra keen can reach the top by doing the 'Grouse Grind', a trail of approximately 2,680 steps. Only the fit and determined are advised to attempt it and it is best to do that during the warmer months. The day before

BOUND FOR VANCOUVER

Christmas in 1949 was definitely not in one of the warmer months. Young Duncan, who was on shore leave from the Aorangi, wanted to see everything Vancouver had to offer and the top of Grouse was high on his list. But there was a problem. His apparel consisted of a pair of jeans, shoes, a shirt and a light pullover. He didn't think twice as he settled in while the chairlift took its leisurely time to arrive at the top. Along the way it offered a bracing climate experience for patrons as well as an unrivalled view. So bracing was the weather that the Aussie sightseer was unable to get himself off the lift at the top of the mountain. A few kind-hearted workers from the chalet took pity on the frozen patron and plied him with tea and biscuits while they found him a place before the fire. Hypothermia averted, they gave him a parka and sent him back down on the lift with strict instructions to dress for the occasion next time he was in town. They also told him to leave the parka at the bottom of the lift. There are limits to Canadian hospitality and it doesn't stretch to giving a frozen Aussie the parka off one's back.

Body temperature restored to normal, it was time for more sightseeing. Duncan boarded a train in Vancouver – the Canadian Pacific Railway – and rode it across the Rocky Mountains to Banff, Alberta. He got off the train in Banff and caught the next one heading back to Vancouver. All up it was close to twenty-four hours, and through the snow and darkness there was precious little to see. Never mind. It was all part of being a tourist in the vast Canadian wilderness. There was a particular reason he had come to Vancouver – the .22 Marlin rifle. He walked into the Hudson's Bay Company department store to obtain his firearm of choice. There he found the Marlin and was dismayed to find that his budget wouldn't stretch that far. What to do? Coming all that way only to return empty-handed was unthinkable. A Mossberg bolt action .22 was within his price range. Disappointed he may have been about to miss out on his dream, it was an acceptable alternative. He duly bought the Mossberg and proudly carried it on the ship and back home. Dunc still owns that prized firearm to this very day.

It is tempting to wonder, and with some justification: 'A fifteen-year-old boy travelling halfway around the world to buy a rifle – what were his parents thinking?' But consider it for a second or two. Had not Cy Page worked his way to Australia as a fourteen-year-old, found employment and returned to England to answer the call of King and country? Was not Jessie herself a down to earth country girl and well-acquainted with the knockabout ways of family and relatives? Underlying all that was Cy's oft-stated view that life is a matter of 'doing what you want to do and when you find something fulfilling that is what makes life enjoyable'.

With rifle securely stowed, Dunc sailed out of Vancouver's picturesque harbour to return home serving martinis and polishing olives. Once back in Sydney, he left his cabin boy days behind. To this day, he has never returned for another trip up Grouse Mountain, and one is yet to see him go near an olive.

5
JACKAROOING AT MOREE

From the chill of Vancouver to the heat and dust of Moree. That unlikely geographical pairing is worlds apart in just about every way it's possible to be apart. Patience is needed to work one's way through this strange juxtaposition, but it makes sense when you get there. The refugee from frostbite, new rifle in tow, recrossed the equator and returned to the warmer climes of the Antipodes only to find that he had stepped off the ski lift into the mind-warping heat of outback New South Wales. Before finding his way out west Dunc spent a year or two working at Amalgamated Saddlers in Petersham. His choice of transport now shifted from his trusty horse to a motorised conveyance. As soon as he was old enough to obtain a licence, Dunc saved hard and bought himself a British-made Ariel motorcycle. This new form of transport allowed him to arrive promptly at Petersham in time for work. While the Ariel was a lot quicker than Big Red, it was nowhere near as stable. Dunc recalls frequently coming off the bike, particularly when he encountered 'deadly' tram lines – 'get tangled up with them, mate, and you were history'. Today it is easy to forget the importance and prevalence of trams in Sydney's early public transport system.

Dunc survived the pitfalls of commuting to work and was now starting to contemplate a life of working in the country. The decision on a change of setting is absolute proof of Pagey's propensity for never – ever – doing things by halves. Father Cy, who was the starter at Beverley Park Golf Club just behind the St George League's Club, heard of a job going out at Moree. The now seventeen-year-old Duncan jumped at the opportunity to have a go at life as a jackaroo.

Beverley Park Golf Club has a couple of distinguished alumni – Bruce Crampton and Greg Norman served their apprenticeships there. Dunc knew Bruce fairly well and remembers going square dancing with him 'way back in the fifties'. Bruce Crampton went on to have a distinguished career on the Professional Golfer's Association tour in North America. He hit a purple patch in the early seventies when he won fourteen PGA events as well as the Australian Open.

Beverley Park's sleek green fairways were a distant memory when young Duncan stepped out into the heat and dust of Moree. Getting there had been a bit of an ordeal. Dunc rode Big Red into Darling Harbour and put him on a livestock train while he caught a passenger train out west. Moree at the time was an isolated town in the early fifties, but Terry Hie Hie on the Myall Plains was barely a dot on the map. But that was Duncan Page's new mailing address when he hopped off the train and was met by his new boss. Actually, there were two bosses – there was the paterfamilias, a cantankerous eighty-seven-year-old 'old boss' who had sired a slightly less cranky 'young boss' at the time in his forties. The first afternoon on the job seemed the right time to get the greenhorn working. No time like the present. So the 'old boss' loaded his new employee and his horse on his truck and drove them to the Terry Hie Hie property he had established in the 1880s. The expansive sheep and cattle property wasn't as big as some, being only 3,500 acres, but it was unfailingly productive. As testament to the quality of his land, the boss regularly collected prizes for his fine grade fleeces at the Royal Easter Show. That level of success came from the old bloke's determination to upgrade the genetics of his flock. But more about that later.

Grumpy and irascible? That doesn't begin to describe the old bloke. All the same, Dunc recalls the young boss wasn't much of a good-time Charlie either. For them and their new employee it was work. Work and then more of the same. Indeed, as the truck rolled up the property's access road at two o'clock in the afternoon, the travel-weary city bloke was deposited in a nearby paddock, given a hoe and told to start chipping weeds. Dunc laughingly recalls how the hoe's handle conveniently broke just as he was about to be picked up for dinner.

Life for a city lad on at Terry Hie Hie was far from salubrious – flies and the withering heat were only part of it. The food wasn't even close to haute cuisine. Today he remembers it as mutton – stewed, baked, boiled, roasted – for breakfast, lunch and dinner. Augment that dietary staple with boiled potatoes and pumpkin and you had the diet for those in the back of beyond. The menu never varied. No fruit, no fresh vegetables, no wondering what Mum has cooked for dinner; you knew months in advance. It was miraculous that the young station hand avoided scurvy. Luckily for him, by now Pagey had shed his baby fat and was the proud owner of a healthy constitution. Fruit was so scarce and so desirable that once, when the young boss was sent a box of apples, Dunc was reduced to petty theft. One-by-one several of the precious apples would mysteriously disappear into the night. Cruel fate and a parsimonious employer drove the undernourished jackaroo to a life of nocturnal thievery.

Work on the land can be, and often is, onerous. Some of the work the new employee was assigned was worse than onerous but, whatever the task, Dunc was up for it. At times he used Big Red for stock work with the sheep and cattle, but much of his daily work was done on foot. Dunc recalls that he preferred to run between his various daily jobs. When queried about the need to run, he insists that, by running, he could get to his chores in a quarter of the time. One wonders if on his jogs between duties he ever considered that the boss might use the time saved to find more for his keen employee to do? Didn't bother asking that. It's too late anyhow.

Some of the work Dunc was required to do could be stomach-turning. After he had left the property, the old boss gave him a reference that contained the enigmatic words 'he is a good killer'. Apparently killing was a key performance indicator for a competent jackaroo. One of his many jobs was killing, skinning and dressing a sheep and then cutting it into portions. That was bad enough, but the worst of the worst was dragging dead and bogged sheep carcasses out of the many large dams on the property. Often hip-deep in mud, Pagey wrestled with the sodden carcasses only to have them come apart in his hands. The sight and the stench can only be imagined. So there you go. That's life on the land for you – all guts and no glory.

Life on the land did have its diversions. Every Australian has his or her very own special snake story. And after his time on the Terry Hie Hie station, Dunc can tell a couple of beauties. He was tossing hay onto a truck one day and, when the load was built, he climbed up and sat down while the young boss drove back to the sheds. As the junior member of the team Pagey was expected to hop off and open the gates. He would then close it and, while the truck waited, hop back on. At the last gate, as he resumed his seat, Dunc found that he had acquired a companion – a large coiled up brown snake. The snake promptly spotted the human and slid out of sight between the bales. They offloaded the hay in the shed keeping an eye out for the reptile. When they came to the last bale – the one under which the snake just had to be hidden – Dunc recalls the young boss handing him an eighteen-inch stick and saying, 'Here you get him with this while I lift the bale'. Pagey instantly demurred, wisely suggesting that he would need a much longer stick than the one offered.

Quick as they could, the last bale was tossed onto the stack and the snake slithered off the truck to hide among the newly stacked small bales to wait for another day to scare the excrement out of the next bloke to come along. That wasn't the last problem he had with snakes. One evening after another long day of punishing work, Dunc reclined comfortably on his bed in the hut provided for him. Oh yes, the hut. The station owners had assigned him a rundown hut that had seen better days. It did have the singular benefit of fending off the sun and rain (rain? What rain?) but the wind and dust worked their way in through the generous ventilation holes in the slab construction. He remembers his accommodation as definitely substandard to the shearer's quarters, noting that they would have downed tools if they were given something like his. But back to the next snake episode. Pagey was reading quietly when he noticed a snake slithering up the end of his bed. Ignoring his rapid pulse rate, he reached for his trusty twenty-two, sighted it and was about to squeeze off a shot when one of the station's mouse-chasing cats dragged its tail off the bed. A deep breath. A bullet saved for rabbits or foxes and one less ventilation hole in the side of his hut.

JACKAROOING AT MOREE

The old boss had an interesting temperament – one that requires a book on its own – but two brief anecdotes will suffice by way of explanation. He once went down to Sydney and came back home with a brand new Studebaker (an automobile company that, like its buyer from Moree, is now extinct). The trip was uneventful, although when he returned with his new purchase, the old bloke swore profusely and stated that the top gear on his new pride and joy was no bloody good. Further examination revealed that he had driven it all the way from Sydney in second gear. The cranky old bugger was unused to, or unable to manipulate, the intricacies of the car's gear box. It's understandable. After all, if a three gear manual transmission can be tricky, what would he have done with five? Then there is the matter of the five hundred guinea ram. The old boss, for all his personality quirks, was a grazier who knew what he was doing. He intended the five hundred guinea ram (a major expenditure in those days – worth close to twenty thousand dollars today) to be a key part in his plans to increase and improve his annual wool clip.

Did not Robbie Burns write something about the plans of mice and men? Well, this particular scheme went 'gang aft agley' for the old boss in a big way one hot Moree Day. Dunc was working with the young boss in a paddock far away from where the old bloke was drenching sheep. The pricey ram was chief among them. One after another the sheep made their way through the sheep dip – in one side and out the other. Then it was the pride of the flock's turn and that was the moment things went pear-shaped. Dunc and the young boss heard it before they saw it. The old boss was beside himself and yelling at the top of his lungs. From a distance they could just make out a frantically waving walking stick. They rushed over to where he stood. By then he was somewhat calmer and, instead of waving his stick, he pointed to the now defunct prize ram – drowned in the sheep dip. Its wool had become saturated with water and made it too heavy for the poor beast to walk out. The old bloke had no shot of getting the prize ram out by himself because all up, Dunc thinks it must have weighed close to three hundred pounds. Another lesson for the young jackaroo – if life on the land can seem stultifying and dull as dishwater, it can also turn cruel in a heartbeat.

While on the subject of dull and stultifying, Dunc's never less than arduous working week was rewarded by half a day off on Sunday afternoon. This generous concession was accompanied by the strict proviso that he was to chase up the cows and milk them in the morning. And he spent his time off how? Doing what country kids always do – he picked up his .22 and disappeared into the bush to ping away at the foxes and rabbits which were in plague proportion. Not exactly Olympic style shooting, but good preparation all the same. The Terry Hie Hie station also provided the spark for a lifelong interest in weightlifting. Ever the inventive young man, Dunc fashioned some barbells out of wood and started working out. Between his makeshift weights and an insistence on running between jobs, the evolution of an extremely fit young man was now well under way. All the same, the demands of the daily workload took their toll. He remembers that after being awakened at four am to go mustering he was fighting off sleep most days. 'Fall asleep mate and you fall off your horse.' To combat fatigue, he took to waving a small gum branch around his head – anything to keep himself awake. Whenever they took a break for smoko, Pagey recalls he would lean his back against a tree and fall asleep instantly.

If all good things must come to an end, thankfully, not-so-good things also don't last forever. Not for a minute does Pagey speak of his days on the Myall Plains as a time of unhappiness despite the less than optimal working conditions. He insists that at the time he didn't really know any better. It was a time in his life when he was up for anything. He is philosophical about his employer and to this day doesn't regard him as unusually harsh. 'It's just the way things were then mate', he says. 'He was nothing unusual. In fact, he was quite normal. It was hard out there and the hard survived.' After more than a year of near-indentured labour, the jackarooing days came to an abrupt end when a letter arrived at the station. It seems the Federal government had need of his services. Duncan was bound for national service or 'Nasho' as it was known at the time. Dunc showed the letter to the old boss who immediately said, 'Don't you worry about that son, I can get you off it'. Not exactly what Dunc wanted to hear so he respectfully declined the offer, hopped on a train and was off to serve Queen and country.

Big Red, his faithful horse, was reluctantly handed over to a relative of the family. To this day Dunc deeply regrets leaving him at Terry Hie Hie to face an uncertain fate.

6

OVERCOMING HURDLES

The long train ride from Moree ended at Central. Then it was another train to Kogarah and a bus to Blakehurst. Home had never looked so good. Cy shook his hand and Jessie welcomed her darling boy with open arms and some special home cooking. No mutton on the menu whatsoever. Hot and dusty Moree, where the birds fly backwards to avoid the dust, was behind him now. Ahead was the path leading to Mexico and Tokyo, but a few hurdles (literally) still had to be cleared. Most pressing was the small matter of National Service. A couple of days at home and then it was time to report first to the Arncliffe Depot and then out to Ingleburn Army Base. The young soldier was assigned to a platoon and there he stood – Duncan McIntyre Page, slouch hat and all.

The first thing Dunc mentions about his Nasho days is 'you didn't learn anything'. He was at Ingleburn for three months straight and then it was weekend duty once a month for two years. He recalls doing 'jungle training' at the Singleton Army Base in the depths of the Hunter Valley. Those who are familiar with that fine town, surrounded by coalmines, know that it bears no resemblance to the deepest Congo. Pagey laughingly recalls being promoted to acting lieutenant on one occasion. The promotion was necessary since every officer above him from corporal to lieutenant was unavailable for service that weekend. Things like that can happen in the Army Reserve. The next day after the absentees showed up the acting lieutenant was busted back to the ranks. Dunc had one brush with fame during his Nasho days. He served with Peter Provan, brother of Norm who later became Dunc's captain in the St George Rugby League side. Peter later went on to captain the Balmain Tigers.

Pagey's time in Nasho was not entirely wasted when he was introduced to the manly art of fisticuffs. He had always been interested in boxing and remembers avidly reading everything he could about the lives of famous boxers. After all, he wasn't too far removed from the glory days of the Maitland

Marvel – the great Les Darcy. Dunc has no idea why, but for some reason he stuck up his hand and entered the battalion championships. He sardonically admits to being 10 stone 6 of fistic fury. They shoved him and another bloke into the ring and said, 'go for it'. Dunc acknowledges that he was pretty quick and, after his stint at Moree, extremely fit. His pugilistic technique was to poke out a left hand and move quickly out of range. He says that in all honesty he 'didn't think the other bloke landed a punch'. That was fine by him. He had a second fight which progressed much the same way. After that Pagey retired from the ring undefeated. 'Boxing wasn't for me mate. I wasn't keen on getting hit, and I certainly didn't like hitting other people.' Ironically, in the Inter-Battalion championships that followed, one of the boxers he had defeated went on to win the whole thing.

If Dunc's breakthrough moment in the world of sport wasn't to be in the boxing ring, there was always the Battalion sports. Keen young National Service soldiers were encouraged to compete in Battalion and inter-Battalion athletic contests. Duncan Page first put a foot on a proper track when he competed in the 880 yards event. Australia was building an enviable record in distance running during the fifties and beyond with names like John Landy, Ron Clarke and Al Lawrence garnering well-deserved headlines. In Landy's case, you could toss in the world record for the mile. Dunc shakes his head in bewilderment at his naivety when it came to preparation and training. He ruefully confesses, 'I didn't know anything. My event, the 880, seemed to be a long distance to me so I was extra careful in my preparation on the day. I walked very slowly to the starting line in order to conserve energy. No warm up. No stretching. Nothing at all.' Hardly recommended procedure for an athlete getting ready to bust a gut. In his first ever race Pagey shot to the front and stayed there to the finish. It was his first athletic event and his first win. After the race Dunc admits that he could barely move. Obviously, there was no warm down.

The impressive wire-to-wire victory in the 880 came to the attention of a fellow competitor, Ron Shoveller, who took out the 100 yards event. Ron approached Dunc and suggested he might like to have a run with the St George Athletic Club. Pagey thought that was a pretty good idea, so he did. Interclub athletics was hugely popular at the time – he recalls that there were eight clubs competing on Saturdays at the E.S. Marks Athletics Field. Sadly, not all competitors were allowed to scorch the cinders at Marks. In keeping with the custom of the times, women athletes were required to compete separately at the old Sydney Sportsground. One can only conjecture about the untold damage male egos would have suffered had Betty Cuthbert, Marjorie Jackson and Shirley Strickland been allowed to occupy the same training facilities as the men. Unisex or not, Duncan Page took to athletics like the proverbial duck to water.

After a few runs with St George, Dunc was approached by the trainer Ernie Watson who had spotted his potential. Ernie invited him to attend training at Kogarah Jubilee Oval on Tuesday and Thursday evenings, '5 o'clock sharp' as Dunc remembers it. It was with Ernie Watson that he first started serious training for hurdle events at distances of 220 and 440 yards. Ernie Watson himself was no slouch as a hurdler having won a state championship in the high hurdles. Under the tutelage of his volunteer coach Dunc's athletics career took off on an upward trajectory. He recalls winning several hurdle events at inter-club meets – 'Never the 110 high hurdles, mate, my legs just weren't long enough!' Always on the lookout for improvement, Dunc opted for another coach and a different training venue. Why another coach? Well it seems he had done a lot of reading about the training routines of European athletes like the great Czechoslovak, Emil Zátopek. Not that he wanted to train in army boots like Zátopek is alleged to have done, but Pagey instinctively knew that he needed to train a lot harder. The Europeans were doing more than twice the work he was putting in and, if he was to continue to improve, he knew that he had to match that. It was time to find a different way. As for the army boots, I checked with Pagey to make sure he didn't resort to training in them. But he did. He found the boots he had been given at Nasho, put them on and ran across the soft kikuyu grass at Carss Park in Blakehurst. That's Pagey. He was going to work as hard as the Europeans all day every day!

Dunc freely admits that when it came to establishing an effective training routine, he had no idea how to proceed. For him, it was little more than catch-as-catch-can and entirely ad hoc. He made things up on the run – literally. It didn't matter where – Jubilee Oval, Carss Park or E.S. Marks – he wanted to run and run every day. 'I didn't know anything in those early days, mate. I just wanted to compete.' When asked, 'Why the hurdles?' Simple answer – the options were extremely limited. The people he trained with at Jubilee Oval were hurdlers, including Ernie Watson his coach. So Pagey went along with the crowd and became a hurdler. That was fine with him because it filled his need to compete and improve. In the end, it was his incredible adaptability and determination that made him unstoppable – starting out as a distance runner, then a hurdler, then a sprinter and ultimately a pentathlete.

With Nasho commitments diminishing and a steady job at the saddlery Dunc could fully concentrate on athletics. He found yet another new coach in the former Hungarian Olympian, Gabor Gerö (invariably called 'Garbo' or 'Garb' by Australians), who was a sprinter who competed at the 1928 and 1936 games. To say the least, Gábor proved an unusual mentor for Duncan. He didn't coach his protégé directly but gave him strict training schedules over the phone. Dunc rang him every afternoon to receive his running orders and then showed up at Rushcutters Bay which he says was 'a magnificent place to train'. The real attraction, he soon realised, in addition to the natural setting was the wonderful camaraderie that developed among the athletes. 'Terrific fellows' is how he describes them today, 'a pleasant group of blokes'. Prominent among them were the Olympians Al Lawrence, Keith Ollerenshaw and Geoff Goodacre as well as many others – including the infamous Kingsgrove Slasher. More about him later.

One training associate of Pagey's who must not be overlooked is Gary Bromhead, another protégé of the never present Gabor Gerö. Gary was a fine sprinter, 100 and 220 yards but a dreadful trainer. In fact, he simply couldn't be bothered to train at all. He would show up, have a chat and go home when the others were finished. In a quiet moment one evening at Rushcutter's Bay, Gary took the time to outline his training regime to Dunc. In essence, Pagey remembers, 'Gary said he liked to move his legs quickly so people would think he was working hard'. According to Dunc, Gary had great ability – 'the man could run'. There was the day at E.S. Marks when he was beaten in the 100 by the reigning world record holder 'Hustling' Hec Hogan. Hec won the event easily. Gary was mightily unhappy with his own performance. He approached Hec to explain the reason for his loss. The victor listened in astonishment to Bromhead's explanation which went like this – Gary told him that he had lost because he was running from north to south and that was uphill and there was no way he, Gary, can run uphill. There were looks of astonishment all around; after all the cinder track at E.S. Marks was as flat as a tack. But Gary was insistent and badgered Hustlin' Hec into having a go in the other direction. Hogan obliged, and guess who won? Well it wasn't the world record holder. Gary Bromhead strutted away feeling entirely vindicated. The spectators were rendered speechless.

Pagey laughs as he recounts the story. 'I'm afraid Gary was scattered aces, but all in all he was a good fellow.' Dunc went on to tell another story about Bromhead in the 220 NSW state championship. Gary was in lane one, the inside lane, and it had been torn up by the competitors in earlier events. Gary expressed his dismay to Dunc who advised him to run on the smoother surface at the extreme outside of lane one. The 220 has a staggered start and when the gun went off, Bromhead's good intentions of staying in his lane (as the competitors are required to do) went west. He veered into lane four which was occupied by none other than Kevan Gosper, himself a formidable athlete. Gosper, of course, was the man who later went on to become the Sydney Olympics supremo. Bromhead's precipitate swerve meant that he had given the field a nine to twelve yard start. He dug in and started to mow down the opposition. According to Dunc, Gary had an amazing finishing burst and he ran past Gosper 'like he was standing still'. But athletic authorities, being what they were and whose chief pleasure seemed to be to strut about ostentatiously in their blazers, were having nothing to do with Gary Bromhead's outrageous conduct. The very idea of changing lanes is not to be tolerated. After much huffing and puffing on the part of the blazers, Gary was disqualified and Kevan Gosper declared the winner. To his great credit, Gosper declined to accept the award.

Gary was the kind of person who was prone to episodes of bizarre behaviour and they caused much merriment among his running mates. He would jog from E.S. Marks to Centennial with the rest of the gang until they came to what Dunc remembers as a structure that looked like a ticket box located on the other side of Anzac Parade. Bromhead would jog across the road to sit in the shelter until the others returned from their run. He would then jog across the road and join in as if it was the most normal thing in the world. The behaviour that ultimately confirmed his eccentricity was when he and Dunc were invited to Bathurst to compete in an athletics event – the celebrated The Carillion Carnival. The moment that forever stands out for Pagey is in the 440 where Gary cruised up to him at the 220 mark and then disappeared from view. Dunc went on to win the race easily and later spotted his mate slowly walking toward him with spikes in hand. 'What happened Gary? Did you do a hammy?' Dunc was genuinely and innocently concerned. 'No mate, it just got too hard, so I stopped.' And there you have the enigma that was Gary Bromhead.

Duncan's athletic career seriously took off once he put the haphazard advice of Gábor Gerö behind him and a new trainer emerged. It was yet another long-distance arrangement because the new guru, Doug McBain, lived in the Blue Mountains. Distance did not hinder the relationship because the new trainer was happy to write out training schedules and send them through the mail. Doug McBain was an academic whose ideas were instrumental in improving the performances of numerous athletes during that era. He was the first to introduce Pagey to the concept of interval training. Dunc retains copies of Doug McBain's detailed training schedules to this day. McBain's correspondence school for athletes resulted in some significant accomplishments. One of his protégés, Percy Hobson, the Boy from Bourke, became the first Indigenous Australian to win a Commonwealth Games gold medal. Percy took out the high jump event in the Perth games of 1962. If Duncan had to endure the wearing of army boots while training at Carss Park, Percy Hobson did it even harder out at Bourke. Most of his training was done in his backyard where he worked on his technique by falling onto a pile of carefully placed wood chips in the punishing outback heat. Only when he competed at significant events was Percy allowed the luxury of landing on rubber mats. Australia's men and women athletes of that distant era had to put up with considerable hardship if they expected to succeed.

Despite the advice of a series of mentors, Dunc believes that the greatest impetus to his personal improvement occurred during the Sunday runs when he tagged along with the other athletes from E.S. Marks. The eclectic group of like-minded individuals would gather for a convivial jog from Kensington over to Centennial Park. He fondly remembers the never-ending banter and laughter. 'They were all terrific fellows and there was great camaraderie among all of us.' It was during these Sunday jogs that he rubbed shoulders with athletes of outstanding ability – some of national and international standing. Athletes who were household names, like Keith Ollerenshaw, Geoff Goodacre and Allan Lawrence. Dunc particularly enjoyed the company of Al Lawrence, a superb distance runner and the world two-mile record holder. In equal measure, Al possessed a wicked sense of humour and a disdain for authority. Another of the blokes Dunc ran with at Centennial Park, and later competed against, was Geoff Goodacre, a world class hurdler. Geoff would later break Jesse Owens's world record in the 220-yard hurdles. Running second to Geoff in that event was none other than Duncan Page. The young man in a hurry was making significant strides in the world of athletics.

It would be remiss not to mention Al Lawrence's role in the identification and ultimate apprehension of the Kingsgrove Slasher. David Scanlon was a member of the St George Athletics Club. Dunc describes him as 'just a club runner' and a 'mediocre distance runner'. But David Scanlon, in his private moments, achieved notoriety as the Kingsgrove Slasher – Australia's homegrown version of Jack the Ripper. Fortunately for local residents, the Slasher never got around to killing any of his victims but his depredations terrorised St George and Canterbury neighbourhoods during the mid-fifties. The Slasher's modus operandi was to enter a house through an unlocked window by ripping through the fly screen with a knife or razor blade. He never sexually assaulted his victims, preferring to limit his perversion to cutting off their pyjamas or nightgowns, and then often leaving them neatly folded at the end of the bed. Occasionally he would leave slash marks on the bodies of his sleeping victims. This creepy individual ran amok in the laissez-faire Sydney of that era where suburban doors and windows were rarely locked. Dastardly David Scanlon was finally run to earth by Detective-Sergeant Brian Doyle of the New South Wales Police. His nephew, Peter Doyle, wrote an account of the Slasher's reign of terror in his book *Stranger in the House*. In an unpardonable oversight Peter Doyle fails to mention the vital part Al Lawrence played in the apprehension of the dreaded Kingsgrove Slasher.

Scanlon was a runner. Dunc describes him as 'more a hanger-on' who showed up occasionally for the Sunday jogs with the crew at Centennial Park. After his arrest, his general fitness explained his ability to stay one jump ahead of the law. On further reflection, Allan Lawrence may have been the first to identify the elusive Slasher. The boys had finished their Sunday run and were in the process of changing in the dressing shed at E.S. Marks. Dave Scanlon was quietly minding his own business when Al Lawrence, ever the boisterous larrikin, looked over at him and said in a booming voice, 'They nearly got you last night mate'. Everyone knew what Al was alluding to and the room resounded with laughter. After the merriment abated no one thought anything more of it. It was just Al being Al. Once the Slasher's identity was revealed Pagey recalls Al saying that poor Scanlon initially went white as a sheet when he accused him in the dressing shed. Only after he was put behind bars did anyone recall the significance of the insignificant incident. Regrettably, by the time the bloke was incarcerated it was too late for the prescient Al Lawrence to receive a police medal.

These early years as a developing athlete were the precursors for Duncan Page's ultimate road to the Tokyo and Mexico Olympics. The life-changing association with Don McMiken and Peter Macken waited just around the corner. Before he could join his mates, a series of major obstacles cast a shadow over his dream of wearing the green and gold.

7

SOMETHING WENT 'WHAM'

The Australia of the 1950s, even in rapidly growing post-war Sydney, retained a strong sense of community; and athletics occupied a prominent place in its social fabric. Television was yet to glue people to their lounge chairs – it didn't arrive until 1956. Prior to that people found their entertainment in many forms – attending the regular suburban athletics meetings was prominent among them. Each club would stage a meet; for instance, St George would invite all clubs to Jubilee Oval where they would go at it hammer and tongs. The meetings were held on weekday evenings and were extremely well attended. Early on in the piece, when he was 'just a kid', Dunc recalls an amusing incident at Hurstville Oval. The then Olympic sprint champion, Fanny Blankers-Koen from the Netherlands, was competing in the 100-yard event. Australia's best at the time, Marjorie Jackson, 'The Lithgow Flash' lined up against her. The home crowd was delighted when Marjorie stormed past the Dutch champion to win. After the race the excited spectators milled around the competitors. Among them was the young Duncan Page. He too was caught up in the jubilation. Ms Blankers-Koen's husband, decidedly annoyed by his wife's unexpected defeat, took it upon himself to clear some space around her. First to attract his attention was young Duncan Page. The unamused husband grabbed the juvenile offender by his shirt collar and the seat of his pants and tossed him out of the way. Such was the lad's first brush with fame.

Dunc's training regime showed serious improvements after Doug McBain took control – 'a really good fellow who went out of his way to help'. After much thought and a long period of dissatisfaction under Ernie Watson and the others, he just had to bite the bullet. It was time for a change. With McBain's schedules guiding his daily routine, Pagey 'religiously' adhered to his mentor's guidance while he trained alone at Carss Park. So religiously and so rigorously did he follow them that he twice broke his foot on the unforgiving ground.

Undeterred by these minor incidents, Dunc gave his feet time to heal and pushed on. His second placing when Geoff Goodacre broke Jesse Owens's 220 hurdle world record caught the eye of the state selectors. They added Dunc to the NSW team to compete in the Australian championships held later that year in Adelaide. Ever the individualist and always adaptable, for reasons he cannot explain today, Pagey took exception to the look of his team blazer which had AAA (Amateur Athletics Association) of NSW on it and had it changed to NSW AAA. Labelling aside, Dunc competed strongly in Adelaide, winning his heats in the 220 and 440 hurdles. In the final of the 440 he led into the last hurdle only to fall and allow the bloke in the next lane to run through. Geoff Goodacre took out the race and Duncan wound up running second to him (again!). On the strength of his strong performance in the final, Pagey was added to the train on squad for the '56 Olympic team. Full of optimism and as fit as he had ever been, the aspiring Olympian lined up for a start in the Labour Day Sports meeting at Redfern Oval.

For many years Australian athletics was bedevilled by the men in blazers. Sports administrators were never happier than when they were able to assert their authority over the athletes who were doing all the work. And they seemed to delight in exercising this authority largely because it was there for them to use. Duncan laughingly recalls a boneheaded blazer blunder during the Adelaide meet. Dave Stephens was a world class distance runner – three to six miles – good enough to be invited to compete in Hungary; a country then aligned to the Communist bloc. Dave was a Victorian who came under the tutelage of the wildly eccentric Percy Cerutty. He had acquired the nickname of 'The Flying Milko' because he made a quid from his milk run in the Melbourne suburb of Footscray. When Dave was invited to compete in Hungary, he was astonished at the red carpet treatment he and the other athletes received. He was provided with all the care and attention he could possibly ask for. He couldn't help but notice that it was laid on with a trowel in that allegedly poor communist country. While competing in Eastern Europe The Flying Milko came under the influence of Emil Zátopek and was delighted when he was given the opportunity to train with the great man for a few days. During his time there, the Hungarians couldn't do enough for Dave and his family. The treatment he received was worlds apart from what he received in his own country where little was on offer. After Australian athletes were selected, Dunc says, 'It was a handshake if you were lucky and then you were on your own'. He jokes about it now but admits that things were diabolical at the time. Athletes were left to their own devices when it came to their training schedules. When it came to financial support, they had to fend for themselves.

It was a typical stinking hot Adelaide day. So hot that Dunc and his mate, John Cann, sat under the cold showers before they went out to compete. They scoffed when they noticed that even during the day's blistering heat, the self-important people never took off their blazers. Unfortunately, their official attire didn't stop them from right royally stuffing things up. Dave Stephens and the other competitors in the six-mile race were scheduled to run at one pm – just when the sun had reached its zenith. The temperature was 115 degrees Fahrenheit (46 Celsius) and everyone who could found a spot in the shade. But there was no shade for the competitors – rules were rules, and the meet must go on. The Flying Milko, treated like visiting royalty in communist Hungary, landed with a thud on home soil. And Dave didn't like it one bit. With each lap of the race, all twenty-four of them, Dave abused the absolute tripe out of the blazer boys when he ran past them. His intemperate language cuts strips from their thick hides. The august gentlemen became increasingly indignant that a lowly athlete had the cheek to challenge them. The race schedule would be adhered to irrespective of weather conditions. Their decision was final and, as a token of their absolute authority, were they not seated under a sheltering umbrella?

Dave went on to win the race but owing to his tirade of ill-disciplined language he was called before the committee. The stuffed shirts were outraged that their judgement could come into question by a mere athlete. So annoyed that they seriously considered denying Stephens (officials always used last names) his medal. After he cooled down, the irate runner was required to account for himself. Dave fronted up and by way of apology confessed that the heat must have 'made him go troppo'. His apology was grudgingly accepted. That incident is far from an unusual example of how the powers that be treated athletes during that era. If they could threaten the world record holder for six miles, what lay in store for the Modern Pentathlon boys – Macken, Page and McMiken?

In a meet at Redfern just before the '56 Olympics Dunc decided to have a run in the 880, known then as 'the half mile'. One of the more curious aspects of his athletics career is that Pagey never really got around to deciding whether he was a distance runner or a sprinter. The confusion was understandable because general opinion regarded him as a distance runner. And yet, shortly after escaping from his Nasho commitment, he lined up to compete for St George at an inter-club meet at Hawkesbury. To help St George garner extra points Dunc volunteered to have a go in the 100 sprint. He speaks of it dismissively now as 'only a B Division sprint', but he won handily. After the race, people came up to congratulate him and express astonishment at his victory over the short course. The distance confusion didn't prevent the versatile Dunc from entering the 880 in a meet on the grass at Redfern Oval as a warm up before the Olympics. Dunc recalls the oval as having a notoriously sandy and uneven running surface. He led the race up to the last twenty yards only to step in a hole and, to use his own words, 'something went wham'. Ignoring the acute warning signs from his leg, Dunc limped across the line to finish first. Unluckily, something indeed had gone 'wham' and that something was severe – he had torn the ligament off the bone in his left leg. And that brought a temporary, and decidedly unwelcome, end to a promising athletic career.

Suddenly Pagey was occupying a seat on the sidelines of the biggest thing to happen in Australia since sliced bread – the 1956 Melbourne Olympics. Poor Dunc, as the time-honoured saying goes, 'if it wasn't for bad luck, he wouldn't have no luck at all'. The rest of the populace was abuzz with the knowledge that the Games would put their country front and centre on the world stage. When asked if he felt sorry for himself, he grins and says, 'No mate, when you're young you just roll along'. And so, the wounded warrior went with the flow and shared the country's excitement when he limped into the Melbourne Cricket Ground as a spectator. Luckily for him Dunc was on good terms with many of the Aussie competitors and was able to find his way into the Olympic Village where security was nothing like it is today. Somehow, he managed to obtain tickets to many of the finals and recalls seeing Australia's 'Golden Girl', Betty Cuthbert, take out the 100 metres and Hec Hogan running a solid third to the Americans Bobby Morrow and Thane Baker. In the distance events there were ominous signs of things to come for the Olympics and sport in general. The Russian, Vladimir Kuts, triumphed in the distance races (5000 and 1000 metres). Al Lawrence, who ran a creditable third, later told Pagey that, when they stood on the podium to receive their medals, Kuts had a glazed look in his eye and had to be turned around to face the right direction. Dunc recalls Al saying, 'The bloke didn't know where he was'.

The Olympics had come and gone. Dunc's bung leg still wasn't healing and there was no way he could run on it. The limited medical advice of the time was no help either, so the leg stayed deformed and not fit for purpose. Things were crook. Never an idler or shirker, Dunc went in search of something to do with himself. He had given away his job at Amalgamated Saddlers – 'there were other things to do' – and commenced a new phase of his career as the proprietor of a night driving range. Golf? Pagey? It's hard to bring the two under one roof, but yet again, as he so often did, Cy Page came to the aid of his youngest son. Bill McWilliam, the professional at Beverley Park Golf Club, knew Cy well and had heard that Dunc was contemplating a career change. Bill then came up with a bright idea. Why didn't he and Duncan combine their resources and take up the lease on the driving range just behind the golf club? Sounded like a plan to both of them, and with Cy's wholehearted encouragement, a driving range it was. Duncan ran the business end of things and Bill McWilliam steered clients his way. Nice little earner it was too, and it turned out to be 'the best job I ever had'.

Best job ever? A big statement from the man who went on to become an expert saddler. The joint venture's success was a gold-plated certainty because there were very few night driving ranges in Sydney. To celebrate the gala opening of the range, Norman O'Neill, the test cricket hero from the local St George club, was invited to hit the first ball. And wouldn't you know it – after giving the club head a waggle and addressing the ball – Normie came up with an air swing! Talk about anti-climax. You wouldn't read about it. The bloke who terrorised England in the Ashes was bowled for a duck at the Beverley Park driving range. Fortunately for Dunc and Bill McWilliam the enterprise was a lot more hit than miss. The job came with side benefits – his working hours were six pm to ten pm and that left Dunc with plenty of free time. Unable to train because of his crook leg, Dunc was at a loose end. It was time for a change of direction. He was soon driving down Port Hacking Road, along the Kingsway and straight into the welcoming reach of the North Cronulla Surf Club. Ever the competitor, Pagey wasn't content to spend his hours gazing at the surf from the seawall. So he found something to do with himself.

Before we leave Dunc about to take off on the crest of a wave, another mate from the '56 Olympics, enters the picture. John Cann, Pagey's cold shower mate from the sweltering Adelaide meet. John was a member of the Randwick-Botany Club who often trained with the boys whether at Rushcutter's Bay, E.S. Marks or Centennial Park. Dunc remembers Johnny Cann as a 'real knockabout bloke and a great fellow'. John was an outstanding athlete – 'good at everything'. He ultimately wound up representing Australia in the Decathlon at the Melbourne Olympics. As evidence of his all-rounder status, John played on the wing for New South Wales in rugby league and was the state light-heavyweight boxing champion. As a boxer he had the distinction of being beaten by fellow Aussie Tony Madigan, who in turn had the distinction of winning bronze at the 1960 Rome Olympics. The gold medallist that year was the young Cassius Marcellus Clay who went on to make something of a name for himself as Muhammad Ali.

Today Dunc laughingly recalls the time at E.S. Marks while he and Johnny watched a 220-hurdle event which a GPS (private school) competitor won handily. The two spectators, dressed casually in their shorts, t-shirt and thongs, watched on while the winner strutted through his warm down. John instantly took a dim view of the private school boy's posh ways. He turned to Dunc and, in a voice full of disdain, said, 'I can beat this bloke'. As fate would have it, at a meet the very next weekend he did just that. He won and won easily. It makes a good story – the boy from La Perouse taking out the well-polished GPS champion. To complete the story, later on that season Dunc ran against the same GPS hero in the 220 hurdles and cleaned him up also. John Cann was another contributor to the sprinter/distance runner confusion that haunted Dunc. A 100-yard hurdle match race between John Cann and another crack hurdler by the name of John Lester was scheduled. The two Johns approached Dunc and asked if he would have a run to make up the numbers. Pagey was happy to oblige and – surprise, surprise – he took out the race. Sprint or distance? The matter was never satisfactorily resolved because the unstoppable Dunc was entirely comfortable competing in both spheres.

There was another aspect to the life of John Cann. His father, George, was the herpetologist at Taronga Zoo. In layman's language, he was a snake handler who regularly conducted demonstrations at La Perouse or the La Pa Loop as it was known to the locals. As befits a good son, John, along with his brother George, followed his father into the family business. There is a knowing look on Dunc's face when he says, 'You always had to watch yourself when you were with Johnny Cann. There was bound to be a snake around somewhere.' He recalls a trip back from a pistol shooting competition in Victoria when, impoverished pentathlete that he was (as they all were in those days) he was bludging a ride home. Pagey, who was chronically broke, had no way of getting back to Sydney other than hitch-hiking. Some kind soul dropped him off outside of Tumbarumba and Dunc was standing on the side of the road waiting hopefully when a vehicle came to a screeching halt beside him. Out from the driver's door stepped John Cann with a beaming smile. The boys exchanged greetings and cordial handshakes. 'What are you doing here mate?'

A wide grin and then, 'No mate what are *you* doing here?' John cheerfully offered his mate a lift saying, 'Jump in Dunc, I'll get you home'. Pagey opened the door, stared inside for a nanosecond, and then froze. There, on the floor of the passenger side rested three hessian bags – sugar bags as they were commonly known. It was a custom of snake handlers, and it continues today, to transport reptiles from place-to-place in hessian bags. Dunc was having nothing to do with the bags or their contents. 'I'm not getting in that car with you Johnny. I know what's in those bags and I'm not going anywhere near them.' Dunc, who has a healthy aversion to snakes of any kind, balked at the idea of putting his feet in their vicinity for several hours. John, who was well aware of his mate's phobia, let out a deep chuckle, came around to the passenger side, grabbed one of the suspicious bags and tipped the contents onto the side of the road. In a heartbeat, Dunc was ten yards away before he felt safe enough to look back. And there, standing over a pile of black muscat grapes, was the hugely amused John Cann. It turns out he had been picking grapes down south and was heading home with the fruits of his labour.

There has to be one more story for the road. One last John Cann tale – and it is a tale that needs telling. The Cann family housed their performing reptiles in a deep pit that was purpose-built in the middle of their backyard. One can safely assume that the household remained untroubled by burglars and, luckily for the Kingsgrove Slasher, it was outside the range of operation. Security system by snake pit? Maybe not. The idea was never going to hit the big time. In truth it was only designed to allow the father George Cann and his two boys easy access to the star performers in their show. The backyard pit-cum-snake house was occasionally put to other uses. Legend has it that John did some of his decathlon training in his backyard. The story may be entirely apocryphal but there are those who insist that he improved his pole vault technique by vaulting over the family snake pit.

John's athletic career came to an inevitable end but his interest in reptiles remained. The La Perouse show finally ended in 2010 but by then John had established himself as a conservationist and a world authority on turtles. He went on to become curator of reptiles at Taronga Zoo, wrote several books and ultimately was awarded the OAM for contributions to his community. Not a bad result for a knockabout lad from La Pa. Pagey, who has an inborn ability to enjoy the company of people from all walks of life, expresses one exception to the general rule: he is extremely wary of any bloke who is carrying a sugar bag.

To complete this period of Duncan's athletic career there was a sunny Sunday at Sydney University – he thinks it was Oval 2 – where he was having a quiet chat with his St George Athletic Club teammate, Albie Thomas. The incapacitated Pagey was hobbling around the oval, unable to keep away from the sport he loved. He stood disconsolately on the sidelines – an unwilling spectator at a major competition. Albie, who was scheduled to compete later in the day, spotted his teammate and wandered over for a quiet chat. When it came to middle- and long-distance running in that era, Albie was pretty much the cream of the crop. He competed at several Olympics and Commonwealth Games and set several world records. Side-by-side the two men talked quietly while the competition whirled around them. Albie asked Dunc how his injury was healing. 'Not real good', was the honest response. Albie said something appropriately sympathetic and Dunc clearly recalls himself replying, 'Ah well Albie, there's always next year'. The pity is that, for the promising sprinter/distance runner, the next year he spoke about never came.

Roughly forty years later, Pagey and Albie Thomas caught up with each other when they shared a room at St George Hospital. They were both in for a relatively minor procedure and were delighted to reconnect. Their nurse was attending to them when the irrepressible Albie piped up, 'Nurse, I'd like to introduce you to a member of my family'. He nodded toward Duncan who wondered what Albie was going on about. The nurse looked quizzically at the elderly men, unable to make the connection. Then, with a wide smile, Albie explained himself, 'Yes, nurse, we are members of the same family, we are members of the Olympic family'.

8

BEACH SPRINTS AND SURF BOARDS

Surfing first came to prominence in Oz when the legendary Hawaiian, Duke Kahanamoku, brought his mighty board with him and demonstrated his skills at Freshwater. The Duke, the 1912 Olympic 100 yard freestyle swimming champion, was invited to Australia in 1914 for a series of exhibition swims. He also remembered to bring his surfboard, which after the fashion of the times, was little more than a finely tuned plank. The board was so big that it would have decapitated swimmers in the vicinity when he came off. Apart from the publicity the great Duke lent the sport, Australian surfers at the time were using planks not too dissimilar from his. What is indisputable is that the feats of the highly admired Hawaiian reinvigorated the sport of surfing in the minds of coastal Australians. In 2014 to mark the centenary of his visit, a statue of the Duke was erected and today it stands proudly above Freshwater Beach.

Now we fast-forward to the late fifties and the seawall at North Cronulla Beach. By the time Dunc arrived at North Cronulla, surfing was so mainstream that even 'Westies' (citizens of the Western Suburbs of Sydney) were getting on trains with towels and boards in hand and hopping off at Cronulla Station. They went straight to the beach starting with Cronulla Beach at the southern end and fanning out in a northerly direction to Elouera and Wanda. Some would even venture as far north as Green Hills. Duncan Page, broken down potential Olympian, now faced the prospect of becoming just another might-have-been. But better things awaited him. As always, Dunc found a silver lining among the massive clouds hanging over his sporting future. After all, there was the driving range and all those daylight hours with which to occupy himself. The logical thing, he decided, was to spend them at the beach.

It sounded like a plan to the bloke sitting on the seawall at North Cronulla. As happened more than once in his life, the good old Yanks came through for him. Pagey had an uncanny ability to be in the right place at the right time. North Cronulla was the obvious spot to commence his love affair with the surf. It was the first beach he arrived at after driving down the Kingsway and turning left into Elouera Road. The allure was obvious. If he couldn't run, he might as well head straight for the beach and into the surf. And that's exactly what Dunc decided to do. In no time, he was intently focused on finding and catching the perfect wave. The impetus came about after he saw a demonstration of surfing skills off the point at Cronulla Beach. The American surf lifesaving team had come north to Sydney after competing at a surf carnival in Melbourne. Off the point at Cronulla they showed off their unique skills on ten-foot Malibu boards. Aussies were accustomed to their sixteen-foot boards and what the Yanks did on their smaller more manoeuvrable boards created a sensation. One look at the smaller boards and Duncan was hooked. From then on, he became the genuine article – a blond-haired real gone stompie wompie surfer boy who somehow never caught up with Little Pattie.

Dunc is convinced that the show the American surfers put on was 'the beginning of board riding in Australia as we know it today'. Duke Kahanamoku had brought his board fifty years earlier, but it was a lethal weapon that weighed close to ninety pounds (slightly more than forty kilos). The new generation of Yanks rode much lighter and more manoeuvrable boards with a balsa wood core and a fiberglass coat. Like the Duke's massive plank, the Aussie boards were long and heavy and you rode them mostly in any direction you wanted – as long as it was straight. The American boards, by contrast, were smaller, lighter and could be turned easily in whatever direction the rider wanted. Needless to say, the Aussies were astonished by what they saw at Cronulla. It wasn't long before Dunc and a few like-minded mates turned their energies to designing boards along the lines of what the Yanks were using. Always the innovator, Pagey came up with a design of his own that was a balsa board with three fins. He believes that he and his North Cronulla Surf Club pals are responsible for coming up with an early version of the tri-fin set up. Simon Anderson popularised the tri-fin in the early eighties with his 'Thruster' boards and, as Dunc is happy to concede, 'We needed three fins for stability while the later boys used the three fin idea for manoeuvrability'.

Possibly because of the liberal application of salt water, Duncan was finding that his crook leg was healing. Time had worked in Dunc's favour. Somehow the injury had healed itself and he was now allowed to run, and run quickly. Time in the water may have helped, but so did his brother Clem Jnr. Pagey discovered that in order to run without pain he needed to strap himself up. Conveniently enough, Clem just happened to work for the pharmaceutical company Johnson and Johnson, and one of its products was Elastoplast. Dunc had access to roll after roll of bandages – at mate's rates – and younger brother put them to good use. So good that, 'buying all those bandages from Clem kept me broke'. And so, with a partially mummified leg, Pagey was about to reinvent himself as a beach sprinter.

Before totally committing himself to the cause of speed over stamina, Dunc hung on to the idea of himself as a distance runner just a little longer. There was the surf club's annual Beach Marathon. The course stretched along the strip of sand that extends from North Cronulla Beach up to Green Hills and back – approximately four miles. Percy Cerutti, that most idiosyncratic of athletics trainers, preached the doctrine of establishing one's authority in a race and mercilessly dominating the other competitors right from the start. Dunc came across Percy's idea in something he read and decided to put it to good use in the beach marathon. So off he went, dominating the lead competitors who had already established a brisk pace. What Dunc failed to realise was that the early pacemakers had no intention of staying the distance and intended to drop out after a mile or so. After they peeled off the Cerutti-inspired Page struggled on, by now imposing his will on himself as much as on the others. 'There was just enough left in my tank to take out the race.' In second place was Ted Larsen, 'a really good club man', who had won the event several times previously. Years later they bumped into each other and Ted asked with a knowing smile, 'Do you remember who won that race Dunc?' The reply? 'I did Ted – just!'

At this moment Max Johnson enters the picture. Max was pretty well 'Mr Everything' at the North Cronulla Surf Life Saving Club. In his long association with the club, he fulfilled just about every position there was to fill – most notably as an astute talent scout. By then Dunc, a fully-fledged member doing his share of patrols, had come to know Max well and enjoyed his company. Now that his leg was on the mend, his mind turned to how he could compete at the regular surf carnivals that were held all summer. There was one obvious candidate – the beach relay – a staple event of all surf club competitions. In his role as club captain, the organisational responsibility for the relay fell on Max's shoulders. Consequently, he was always on the lookout for talent to help the club obtain valuable competition points. He was aware that, until he was injured, his new mate had been included in the Melbourne Olympic train-on squad. The canny club captain welcomed Dunc with open arms. He could recognise a decided asset when he saw one; and now that the bloke was fit and healthy, he was certainly one of those. As Max admitted in his comprehensive history of the North Cronulla Club, 'What we needed for the relay was an outstanding performer who could give us the edge'. Max was pretty sure he had found his man in Pagey.

The beach relay is a hotly contested event at surf carnivals. It is a premium event that involves four runners from each club. The competitors are not provided with a flat manicured surface to maximise their explosive speed. Far from it, they have to make do with what the waves washed up. Positions are determined by draw, and potluck determines who gets the better surface. In theory, the closer to the water, the firmer the sand, although the vagaries of Mother Nature are ever a limiting factor. The runners face each other roughly seventy-five yards apart, two at each end and wait anxiously for the sound of the gun. After the starter pulls the trigger the relay comes close to chaos. Blink and you'll miss it. Up and down the stretch of sand the runners go, rapidly handing the baton to the next runner. Careful – drop it and you're gone! The scene is nothing less than frantic – flying sand, flailing arms and a blur of legs until, in an instant, it is over.

The beach relay is a jewel worth coveting, and the North Cronulla boys badly wanted it. The club had a pretty hot team for a couple of years and Duncan recalls how John Riley, a future St George teammate, was an integral member. John, a very quick winger, went on to represent New South Wales and Australia in rugby league. Between him and Duncan (Pagey was the quickest in the team and consequently ran the last leg), North accounted for numerous inter-club victories. But the biggest prize, the Australian interclub championship, had so far eluded them. As for Dunc, it seems that the distance runner/sprinter conundrum was settled at last and he had found his rightful niche – he was officially a beach sprinter.

With wry humour he recounts the story of how his beach sprinting days almost ended before they began. In those days, the first interclub meet of the year was held at Garie Beach deep in Royal National Park. The event was always well attended, and Garie's parking lot was chocka. It wasn't long before the police ordered people to park on Sir Bertram Stevens Drive at least a mile and a half (roughly two kilometres) from the beach. Pagey parked his car and walked along the dirt track that led down to the beach with a couple of other club members. He won his event and, after the meet, started the long walk up the hill hoping someone would offer him a lift. His wishes were answered when a chap stopped and opened the passenger door. The ride didn't last long because (as Dunc found out to his dismay) the highly inebriated driver lost control of his vehicle. He veered off the dirt road and tore through the bush. No seatbelts in those days of course – the car flipped 'a couple of times' and came to rest against a large gum tree which offered a clear view of the Pacific Ocean and a precipitous drop of two hundred feet. Duncan vowed then and there that never again would he get into a car with a bloke who was as 'drunk as a skunk'.

That death-defying episode behind him, Pagey relates, with considerable although appropriately modest satisfaction, an episode during the inter-club meet with arch-rival Cronulla Surf Life Saving Club. Cronulla, the senior of the two clubs, is located one beach to the south of North. It goes without saying that the competition between the two could become extremely willing. Dunc was listed to run in the beach relay as well as the beach sprint – an individual race over the same course as the relay. Lined up against him was Cronulla's Bobby Bugden, the current St George Leagues Club first grade halfback. In addition to his club duties with the Dragons, Bob went on to represent New South Wales and, ultimately, his country in rugby league. He also had the distinction of being the current Australian Beach Sprint Champion. Bugden was quick, cocky and he expected to win. Needless to say, Dunc had other ideas. There is little to recount about that particular race except that it was over in a heartbeat. And the prize was taken out by? Duncan Page first, and the rest can please themselves. Dunc remembers Bugden as a hyper-competitive individual who didn't like being beaten and he didn't try to hide it. Pagey laughs when he says, 'Yes he was pretty cut up about it'. He offers mitigating circumstances by saying that, in his experience, 'Most halfbacks are like that anyway'. That observation is borne out in Larry Writer's *Never Before, Never Again*, the comprehensive history of the St George Rugby League Club's eleven-year winning run. There, in black and white, Bob puts up his hand and confesses that at the time, 'I had a big ego'.

There were many other successes in Dunc's beach sprint career and, of course, some inevitable setbacks. One event in particular comes to mind where once again, courtesy of the boys in blazers, the race at the Sydney Metropolitan Championships got royally stuffed up. Sitting on a three-tier stand, designed specifically so they could clearly see each individual competitor, the officials somehow contrived to overlook the winner of the individual beach sprint. Pagey was a clear winner but for some reason the blazers didn't rate him a place. Dunc knows he won; 'I had a look as I crossed and I won by a yard.' North Cronulla official, Ray Shirley, who had been watching carefully, approached the judges and protested vigorously. And the blazers – the very blokes who hadn't even seen Dunc run? They magnanimously awarded him second place. In the days before instant replays you have to wonder what other atrocities were committed by the partially sighted blazer boys.

The Australian Interclub Surf Lifesaving championships now beckoned. They were held that year at Mooloolaba on Queensland's Sunshine Coast. That was where Dunc realised the crowning moment of his individual surf club accomplishments when he lined up for the beach relay and the individual beach sprint. The beach relay team suffered a major setback when John Riley was unavailable because he was required for duty by St George. Missing one of their vital cogs, the North boys finished second by a hair with Duncan running the last leg. Things were different in the individual beach sprint. Pagey was primed and ready and, after a few brief seconds of flying sand and feet, he was victorious. Duncan Page – Australian Inter-state Beachsprint Champion – not a bad result for a bloke who a couple of years earlier had struggled to walk.

9

THE JERSEY SHORE

A fair bit of water lies between North Cronulla and a dot on the map called Jersey in the Channel Islands. They are called the 'Channel' Islands because that's where they are – in the English Channel just off the coast of France. Because of some quirk of history, they are linked politically to the United Kingdom. Confused? Same here. But I'll leave you to sort out the finer details. Anyway, for reasons best known to a restless young man in search of another adventure, Pagey wound up in Jersey as a lifeguard. He was assigned to protect locals and tourists – mostly from themselves, it turned out. As a fair indication of the swimming proficiency of the Jersey bathers Dunc and his fellow lifesavers came to a mutual understanding. 'We kept a close eye on the swimmers and if anyone of them was in water up to their armpits, we'd go out and rescue them.' The fundamental Australian assumption about Poms and their aversion to water proved true – even in Jersey.

'Why Jersey?' he was asked. 'Why not?' he replied. The siren call of faraway places was impossible to ignore. It was made even more impossible when the Jersey Life Saving Club ran an ad in the *Sydney Morning Herald* inviting applications from Aussie lifesavers. Two blokes from Cronulla and two from North put up their hands. Duncan Page, like the other three, was always up for something new. Sounded like a bit of a lark saving Poms from drowning. So he thought he might give it a go. He sold up his interest in the driving range (something else was bound to come up when he got back) and off he went. Not on a plane, mind you; he and the boys went by ship. The voyage took at least three weeks and somewhere along the way Dunc performed a mid-ocean rescue. One of the Cronulla boys found his way out of the ship's bar and, with a lot on board, attempted to demonstrate his surfing skills on the liner's railing. Pagey, who never developed a taste for alcohol, saw the bloke struggling to find his centre of gravity and quickly deterred him from catapulting to a watery grave.

The boys had a look around when they reached the Suez Canal. After disembarking they took a bus to Suez city. Somewhere along the way there was time for a pit stop so they went looking for souvenirs in the first shop they found. It was a hot day and the Coca Cola was freely available to paying customers. All went swimmingly until they returned to the bus to continue their journey. The driver was ready to pull away when he was stopped by the shop's owner – a menacing looking Egyptian who gesticulated at him with a Lee-Enfield .303 rifle. The driver understood his meaning and turned to face his alarmed passengers. In broken English he informed them that the irate gentleman with the rifle was not going to allow the bus to depart unless and until his Coke bottle was returned. The responsible person (Pagey insists he wasn't the guilty party) sheepishly handed over the half-full bottle and a relieved group of tourists were allowed to continue on their way.

A few hours later they reached Suez and as keen young travellers tend to do, this lot opted for more souvenir hunting. Again, the ever-present Coca Cola played a part in their activities. The Aussie gang of four wandered into a shop and were gratified when the proprietor handed out bottles of Coke accompanied by an ingratiating smile. They wandered around the shop sipping their drinks buying this and that. Some downed all their drink; others were content with just a sip or two. When the spending spree abated and they had wandered off, Dunc realised he had taken his bottle with him. He rushed back to the shop to return it, wanting to forestall another episode of being bailed up by a bloke with a rifle. By then the owner had retired to the back of the shop so Dunc stuck his head around the corner with bottle in hand. The scene he beheld is burned into his memory. There at a table sat the owner's kids, carefully siphoning off the remaining Coke from the partially emptied bottles into another bottle. The full bottle would later be presented gratis, complete with ingratiating smile, to the next unwary customer. Duncan did not say whether he bothered with the famous beverage the rest of his time in Egypt. But he did say that he was 'never so glad as to not bother to take a drink from the bottle they gave him. I must have known something mate.'

It is not a matter of common knowledge, but Jersey has a fair few beaches to patrol so Dunc and the boys were responsible for the most frequented of them. The main beach, called St Brelade, comes complete with a World War II sea wall kindly provided by the Germans and their contingent of slave labourers from the island. At low tide, Dunc says it was possible to walk out at least two hundred yards on the sand. When the tide made its return journey, he enjoyed measuring the water's progress by walking ever so slowly as it crept shoreward. 'The surf was nothing special but now and then you could get a decent wave on a good day.' It is a truism that if you want to catch a wave it helps to have a surfboard. So Dunc set about making himself one. He found some balsawood and got to work. Intrigued by the Aussie's industry, Jersey locals warned him that the surf was 'too rough, too dangerous'. Despite their well-meant advice, the North Cronulla boy kept on shaping and refining his board – the Jersey waves were not going to intimidate him.

The Aussie contingent, backed up by a South African mate – 'The best body surfer I have ever seen' – needed digs and found them in a local pub (what else would young Aussies look for?). The Pembroke Hotel was a venerable old pile that fronted a golf course, and it was there that the Jersey adventure kicked off in a big way. Early in his stay, Pagey walked past the kitchen when he witnessed what he thought was 'almost my first murder'. The hotel's cook, knife in hand, was intent on doing damage to a barmaid who was vigorously defending herself with a chair. Dunc poked his head in the door and roared, 'What's going on here?' That one moment of heroic intervention Pagey insists is the moment he effected his first dry land rescue. The cook, startled into momentary sanity, bolted out the door and was last seen hotfooting it across the golf course. The barmaid? She put the chair down and got on with her work.

But that wasn't the end of the matter. The police had been notified and arrived in due course. Details were taken and, in the manner of a slower time and place, they thought a pint was in order. 'Just the one, mind.' It had been a long drive out of town, wasn't it? The police presence was unknown to the cook who returned in the early hours (still enraged over what Dunc assumes was a jilted love imbroglio), this time to bang on the barmaid's door. He shouted and threatened and made a general nuisance of himself. The constabulary were in the process of finishing off yet another pint (the intention of having 'just the one' went west after the sixth). Upon hearing the unseemly commotion, they lowered their glasses to utter, 'Nah then, nah then, wot's this?' They surrounded the lovesick individual and made a peremptory arrest. Who says business and pleasure cannot be mixed? Back in the day they seemed to go hand-in-hand in Jersey.

Hours of duty for the lifeguard fraternity were normal business hours – nine to six. No exceptions tolerated. The boys positioned themselves along the massive seawall and waited for the unwary Poms to approach their Plimsol line, water up to their armpits. They would then spring into action and retrieve the swimmer from the perilous depths. The Aussies must have been doing something right because that year – 1960 – was the first year there were no recorded deaths by drowning in the beaches off Jersey. But their overseas idyll was never going to last forever. Things were progressing too well. Something had to stuff up – and stuff up they did in fine style. In the backwash of events, Duncan Page had his first and only experience of industrial action.

As is so often the case, the instigators of the Monty Python-esque fiasco that ensued were none other than office bearers of the Jersey Life Guards Club. It all went pear-shaped when one of that breed – a self-styled big player in the club – contrived to leave the club's jeep marooned on the beach. The abandoned vehicle was at the mercy of the tide and was duly submerged by onrushing water. When it was reclaimed the following morning, the rescuers found that the jeep wouldn't start. Surprise, surprise. The guilty party, of course, was the bloke in a blazer, but instead of copping it sweet, he covered his copious arse by blaming it on the Aussies. You hear it all the time – 'The incomers did it'. The thing was, the incomers hadn't done it and they weren't going to wear the blame. But what are you going to do when the blazers gang up on you? The foreigners were outnumbered and, on trumped up charges, they were immediately given the sack. Worse still, they were dismissed without pay. Their response? Down tools and immediately go out on strike. They knew the sentiment, if not the words, of 'Solidarity Forever'. Dunc insists to have it on record that despite the industrial contretemps, all the lifesavers continued to report for duty despite the fact that they were not being paid.

The victimised Aussies may have been outnumbered but they were certainly not outflanked. One of the spurious charges brought against Dunc accused him of leaving his post early one evening. Unfortunately for his persecutors, on the day in question he had been in the company of an attractive English rose, who was the daughter of a massively important British Army general. She presented evidence to the effect that the charge was false and probably vexatious, given that she had been with Dunc that evening and had to wait for him to clock off at – wait for it – six pm. One charge bit the dust courtesy of the Brigadier-General's daughter.

Other charges focused on the Aussies' laissez-faire approach to their duties and their inveterate insubordination. Laissez-faire? Early on in the piece, a blazer came up with a great idea. He thought it would be a fine thing if the lifeguards stood to attention along the seawall at St Brelade while they were on duty. 'Nah mate, don't think so. We'll sit and watch the swimmers if it's all the same to you.' As already noted, the proof of their professionalism was in the results – no drownings that summer. But a chronic disinclination to follow unreasonable directions earned them black marks from the landlubber bigwigs. As for the charge of insubordination – they were Aussies, weren't they? Right from the start the Jersey excursion was destined to end in tears.

Witness statement one: from the local captain of the Jersey Life Guards who also happened to be the local headmaster. That puffed up personage watched a plane take off from the airstrip behind the beach while it tested first one engine, and then the other. Somehow the bloke got it into his head that the aircraft was in danger. He insisted that he and Dunc follow in the jeep. They sped along the beach for a couple of miles until they were blocked by a massive headland. The headmaster vented his frustration at being pulled up and glared at Dunc. The implication being that the geological obstruction was the insubordinate subordinate's fault. Pagey idled the vehicle and tried to suppress a smile. The bigwig's tirade subsided only after Pagey drily inquired, 'What do you want me to do mate, pull back on the wheel and take off? Should I try saying "up, up and away"?' They watched while the plane, clearly no longer in peril, continued serenely along its predetermined flight path and disappeared into the blue. Unwillingness to make a Jeep fly was construed as yet another instance of gross dereliction of duty. For the wannabe Biggles in a blazer it was another black mark against those recalcitrant Australians.

Witness statement two: another grand poobah from the surf club took decisive action one blustery day after spying a freighter struggling against the elements four hundred yards offshore. He ordered Dunc into the club's jeep and together they set off with every intention of being the first Jersey lifeguard to effect a rescue of a seagoing vessel. Over the clamour of the raging tempest, the pompous blazer shouted, 'Take a line and swim out to that freighter'. Dunc declined the offer and, in Eccles' best Goon Show voice, he said 'Oh I get it chief, you want me to swim out there, toss them a line, put it in my teeth and tow the ship back to port.' The response has gone unrecorded, but it is unlikely to have been well-received. The black marks kept adding up.

The unlawful sacking and the industrial action that ensued was headline news in Jersey. Unfortunately for those in charge at the surf club, the storm clouds that hung heavily over the English Channel also threatened their credibility. Today Pagey will happily show you newspaper clippings of the fiasco. The sacking of the four Aussies and their South African mate severely strained normally cordial Commonwealth bonds. The Colonel Blimps in command centre refused to buckle in the face of general outrage. Most of the locals had become fond of the Aussies, and a few even expressed gratitude for having been rescued. The blazers did their best to stand firm, but then they went and shot themselves in the foot. With outstanding judgement, they decided to hire another four lifesavers – this time from the UK. The fundamental problem with that decision was that the new lifesavers had no experience of surf rescue – they were accustomed to supervising swimmers within the limited confines of a pool. The blazers then shot themselves in the other foot by refusing to pay out the sacked Aussies. At that precise moment, everything hit the fan simultaneously.

The boys hired a lawyer to present their grievances before the Jersey court. When their evidence was forensically laid out, particularly the refutation by Duncan's lady friend, his Honour spent approximately five seconds deliberating. When the 'all rise' sounded the beak summarily tossed the case out of court – AWOL, chronic insubordination and drowned vehicle charges included. He then ordered that the Commonwealth brethren were to remain on duty in Jersey until they had fulfilled the remainder of their contracts.

This ignominious defeat left the blazer boys in something of a pickle. They were left with double the number of lifesavers on the payroll for the rest of the season. To compound the humiliating loss in court, the very next day the weather turned foul and remained so for the rest of what is called 'summer' in Jersey. There was little the boys could do but take refuge from the elements in a restaurant overlooking the beach – 'El Tico' it was, and is still called today. Dunc fondly remembers the refuge for its excellent coffee and the vantage point it gave for supervising the beach. The filthy weather refused to abate for the following month. Their employers could only watch on with glowering looks and gnashing teeth while the squalls whirled and the rain lashed at their windows.

The time in Jersey had given Pagey a bad case of itchy feet. His mates weren't all that surprised when he said, 'Hooroo boys, I'm off to Rome'. Before we accompany him to the Eternal City, there remains a spot of tidying up to do. As he narrated this story, almost as an afterthought he asked, 'Have I told you about my mates Johnny Whelan and Nugget Gately?' As a matter of fact, he hadn't. But it seems that Messrs Whelan and Gately were crash hot tennis players and, like many Aussies, they aspired to have a go at Wimbledon. The plan was to play in a couple of qualifying tournaments to see if they could get a game on the big stage. As a plan, it was a goer when they boarded the ship with Dunc and the other lifesavers. They all met up when, after a couple of days, Johnny and Nugget heard familiar accents. Everyone agreed the other were decent enough blokes, so they started knocking around together. Unfortunately for the Wimbledon bound, there was a problem. John and Nugget hadn't properly accounted for the length of the voyage. When they disembarked at Southport, they were dismayed to learn they were two weeks too late to qualify. Ah well, you can't help bad luck. So, with tennis no longer on the menu, they tagged along with their new mates to have a look at Jersey.

Not only could they play tennis, they could also play football and soon, an evening game of touch on the golf course was part of the daily routine. The games were skilfully played and fiercely contested and soon attracted the attention of a chap holidaying in Jersey. The bloke was Mike Hurst, and he just happened to play five-eighth in the Yorkshire representative rugby league team. Mike was particularly impressed by Duncan's skill and speed and suggested that, should he be interested, he, Mike, would arrange a tryout with Wakefield-Trinity, the perennial rugby league champions of Mother England.

Pagey demurred. He was dead keen on Rome and the 1960 Olympics, so he told the Yorkshire man that he would look him up if he ever came back to England. But for now, Rome it was, and more fuel to the fire of Dunc's Olympic dreams.

10

THE ETERNAL CITY

When he boarded the ferry to France, Pagey wasn't traveling solo on his Roman holiday. Nugget Gately, the amiable bushie from West Wyalong, thought he might as well tag along to see what Rome had to offer.

The boys got off the ferry and hopped on the train that would take them to Rome. The city surfie and the back-block bushie watched the panorama of Western Europe flash by. No wide-eyed wonder for those two – by then they were seasoned travellers who took everything as it came. The only incident worth recording was Nugget's inability to find a seat in the carriage. So the big bloke plonked himself down in the dining car and remained there, deaf to repeated requests to camp somewhere else. No matter how the waiters pleaded, Nugget's response was the same, 'I'm not shiftin' mate'. The waiters sized up the obdurate passenger. He was a very large man who looked like he could handle himself and there was no doubt he meant business. For the time being then, Nugget Gately enjoyed the beauties of the Alps while remaining oblivious to the diners scoffing their sumptuous meals beside him.

Rome, ah Rome – the Eternal City. As Pagey recalls with no great fondness, 'It was a hundred plus degrees every day'. But other than the oppressive heat, the city fathers had everything in Rome shipshape and in good order. Dunc got off the train and wasted no time on touristy things – no Colosseum, no Spanish Steps – not for him. It was straight to the Olympic village in search of his mate, Tony Hammet, a reserve for the Modern Pentathlon team. A brief explanation is in order. Even before he left for Jersey, Dunc had commenced a casual flirtation with pentathlon. He could relate to its skill set – riding, shooting? Not a problem. Run? Sure, he could do that. Fencing, swimming? Worry about them later. Before leaving he had even competed in a pentathlon event at Lang Lang in Victoria where, in the run, he finished two seconds slower than the winning time at the Melbourne Olympics on the same course.

UNSTOPPABLE

Dunc's interest in Modern Pentathlon began after a chance encounter with Terry Nicoll. Terry was an Olympic pentathlete and he was renowned for his grandiose opinion of his rather modest abilities. So great were his fabrications and invented exploits that he was universally referred to by fellow competitors as 'Freddy the Fibber'. Dunc wasn't to know this at the time and was immensely impressed when he saw Terry at Scarborough Park near Kogarah. He was impressed by Terry's 'shadow fencing' – lunging, thrusting, parrying and doing whatever else fencers do. He watched respectfully from afar, waiting for an opportunity to have a chat. It took little asking before Dunc was told that Terry was part of the Modern Pentathlon team that competed at the Melbourne Olympics. What fascinated Duncan even more was Terry's assertions about his accomplishments in other spheres. Among other things, Pagey learned that his new mate had been the Australian Buck Jump Champion and had been invited to Russia to teach their pentathletes the finer points of fencing. With those dazzling tidbits of information whirring through his head, Duncan decided he might give the sport a go. He possessed most of the credentials – run, ride and shoot. He could pick up the others on the go. So he entered the event at Lang Lang in Victoria, and that was where he first met his lifelong mate Peter Macken. And there, not for the last time, he ran second to Pete in the run – this time by ten seconds. The run in Modern Pentathlon (in those days) was 4000 metres (the competition always used international measurements). Pagey was fit, but he was now a beach sprinter; not distance fit any more and it showed. All the same, his second placing was encouraging.

The reserve on the Rome pentathlon team, Tony Hammet, was a good mate and he and Pagey shook hands cordially when they caught up outside the village. Tony invited Dunc in, found that there was a spare room and said, 'Why not stay here mate?' From then on, the visitor came and went as he pleased. The hospitality was all-inclusive – showers, bathrooms and, best of all, the cafeteria with its unlimited food. Dunc quickly made a firm friend of the Italian chap guarding the back gate. The guard wondered whether the

Australian gentleman had any souvenirs he could spare. As it so happened, Pagey had a pocketful of Qantas flying kangaroo pins which he generously handed over to the Italian and his extended family. After making a new best mate, it was 'anything you please, for Signor Page'. Although it was a relaxed atmosphere at the Rome Olympics, some level of security was maintained. Dunc remembers walking through the entrance one day with the temperature hovering around a hundred degrees. As he sauntered into the village, he couldn't help but notice the forlorn figure of Vladimir Kuts waiting for someone to let him into the village. It can be a cruel world for former champions, and for Kuts, it was a big come down – rooster in Melbourne, feather duster in Rome.

With access to the Olympic Village now a lay down misere, the boys turned their minds to getting Pagey a pass to all the events. Dunc came across a passport photographer outside the village and had a couple of photos made. With photos in hand, their scam worked like this: Tony Hammet and Peter Macken would enter the stadium. One would come out again with the other's pass and hand it over to Dunc. He would then clip his own photograph over the original and walk through the gate as cool as you like. Today, Dunc shakes his head when he recalls, 'The passes they gave us were only made of cardboard, and in the end we just kept making ourselves another one. Never had a moment's problem with it either.' With access guaranteed, it was straight to the stadium for the track and field events. It was there Dunc watched the incomparable Herb Elliot win the 1500 metres while a wildly excited Percy Cerutty waved him on with his legendary white towel.

Herb's win is the stuff of Olympic legend, and it bears repeating here. The night before the race Percy and Herb sat down to devise a strategy. Percy would be in the stands near the finish line and if Herb was close to a world record or he was threatened by another runner Perce would wave a white towel. It is a matter of historic record that, during the race, in order to get closer to the track so Herb could see him, Percy eluded several stadium guards, crossed a formidable moat and took up a prominent position at the rail. Herb spotted the waving white towel and knew it meant one of two things: he was either in trouble or close to a record. Whatever it meant, he knew he had better get a leg on, so he put in the big ones and finished a long way ahead of the following runner – the largest winning margin in the history of the event. After the race, Percy was apprehended by Rome's constabulary and, as he was more than capable of doing, he managed to talk his way out of serious trouble.

Dunc vividly remembers Herb's spellbinding victory because his forged pass allowed him to see it all: Percy's mad dash to his trackside position, Elliot's withering run down the straight and the white towel waving frantically. Pagey is absolutely certain that the Aussie had the race won before the starter even lifted the gun. In the minutes before the start the competitors congregated and mingled nervously together – everyone except Herb. Dunc watched while he removed himself to stand calmly aloof from the other runners who eyed him nervously. That left Pagey with no doubts, 'When I saw that mate, you could tell the others were running for second'.

In addition to attending all the major track events, Dunc was a keen spectator at the swimming. In the pool, the great Dawn Fraser took out the 100-metre freestyle – an event she went on to own – for the first time. She won the event at the next two Olympics but was incomprehensibly denied a crack at a fourth consecutive victory by the toffs in the blazer brigade. Her crime? In a moment of youthful exuberance, she shinnied up a flagpole and pinched an Olympic flag. Oh, the shame it brought all Australians! For disgracing her country, she was officially ostracised. In the end, it reflected badly on the blazers because it won Dawn universally popularity. She became 'Our Dawn' while the blazers are still just a few long forgotten stuffed shirts.

Duncan had the pleasure of seeing John Konrads win the 1500 and Murray Rose the 400. Murray also finished second to Konrads in the 1500. The big moment came in the men's 100 metre event where the Aussie, John Devitt, won in a blanket finish over the American Lance Larson. At the end of the race, Larson carried on like an A-grade pork chop, by extravagantly expressing his dissatisfaction with the result. Rarely has so much water been splashed to so little effect – not even in a fully occupied toddler's pool. To this day, the Yanks swear they won the race and can cite any number of facts in support of their case. The righteous indignation was unflagging. For years they continued to demand the return of 'their' medal from the Australian Swimmer's Association. All in vain it seems – they would have done well to heed the fine old Australian maxim, 'Winners are grinners and losers can look after themselves'.

After the drama of Larson's spectacular hissy fit, the Olympics slowly wound down and it was 'arrivederci Roma'. Pagey, who was now at a loose end, thought he'd return to England and the Yorkshire town of Wakefield to see if Mike Hurst was as good as his word. So it was back to the Old Dart where he could also catch up with John Whelan. But first he stopped off with his relatives in his father's Essex hometown of Grays. The first day in the house of his kin, he woke to find the place empty – the occupants had departed to their various occupations. Pagey wandered into the kitchen and spied a couple of bananas on the kitchen table. Feeling a trifle hungry, as young men tend to do shortly after rising, he scoffed the bananas down before setting off to see the sights of Grays. When he returned home, he put his head down for a nap only to be woken up by the sound of general distress. A wail emanated from downstairs with the unanswered question: 'Who ate all the week's fruit?' Mortified by embarrassment, the chastised guest found a fruit shop where he purchased a goodly portion of its offerings. He sheepishly returned with arms full of fruit and unobtrusively left them where the now-vanished bananas had been on display. Shortly thereafter, Dunc left for Wakefield, secure in the knowledge that at the very least his relatives would remain free from scurvy for another winter.

It turned out that Mike Hurst had been as good as his word. He had spoken to Wakefield Trinity's decision-makers and told them that when Duncan Page showed up, 'You would be daft if you didn't give this fellow a go'. John Whelan had also received Mike's recommendation and was training with the side when his mate from Jersey arrived. At the time Wakefield Trinity was the gun team in the comp – apart from two players, the Wakefield boys constituted the entire Great Britain side. It was something of a feather in the Aussie's cap to be invited to have a run with them. After training for two weeks, all questions about their future were decisively settled – the boys were in. A fair offer was made and they didn't think twice before signing on the dotted line. The future looked bright – as bright as anything can look in the depths of a Pommie winter.

If Rome is the Eternal City, Wakefield struggles for recognition. That's not to say it doesn't have some fine old buildings – just nothing to match the grandeur of the Colosseum and its fellow relics. 'Mate, it was bleak and grimy and cold', says Pagey. 'A typical coal mining town.' The first night there the boys found a room in a hotel. Dunc took a bath – 'no showers' – and then thought nothing more of it. The next morning a 'most indignant' landlady, her thick Yorkshire accent made thicker with her ire, upbraided the bather saying that, 'all baths have to be booked in advance'. Further problems with personal hygiene were avoided when the kindly Mike Hurst put the boys up for a few weeks until they found permanent digs.

Ultimately the club provided John and Duncan with accommodation in a weary old manor house not far from the ground. They didn't mind its creaking age – it was a roof over their heads and shelter from the Wakefield weather. The house sat next door to an old church, and the church was surrounded by a graveyard. Who knows? The churchyard was probably full of ghosts and the house next door may even have had a spectre or two in residence. 'When you came home on a dark night you rushed into the house and shut the door quick smart', says Pagey. He recalls one particularly spooky the night when they returned from seeing Alfred Hitchcock's *Psycho* in town. Young men do get up to mischief, do they not? Well, Johnny Whelan was nothing if not young and mischievous. The night was dark and windy with a luminous full moon overhead, and John waited for Dunc to retire before he crept up to his mate's bedroom. Duncan was drifting off to sleep when he heard a scratching and shuffling outside his door. Slowly the door creaked open and he saw an apparition in the light of the hallway. Dressed in white and armed with a knife, the ghost slowly glided into the room. The suspense was shattered when the wraith erupted in a fit of uproarious laughter. The unearthly being proved to be entirely earthly – being none other than John Whelan draped in a bed sheet and armed with a bread knife borrowed from the kitchen. The response of the room's now wide-awake occupant has gone unrecorded.

Duncan enjoyed the training at Wakefield and, while there, he put his natural ability to good use. The common practice after a game was for all players to share a common tub – the concept of showering not being customary in that part of the world apparently. The problem with the tub was that the water's warmth rapidly decreased as more players arrived. Dunc happily describes how his beach sprint velocity enabled him to hop in the tub before the lumbering forwards arrived to immerse their large frames. He was in and out before the Wakefield winter chill decreased the water temperature.

Training was always at night. 'It was as black as the ace of spades', says Duncan. The smoggy air was so thick with coal dust that, 'sometimes you couldn't see the fellow next to you. You would have to wear a hankie or a scarf over your nose and mouth and when you took it off, your face was black'. Pagey also recalls that, in that part of the world, the grandstands were built almost on top of the field. Consequently, there was very little gap between players and spectators – a serious disadvantages for the opposing team. 'When you ran out onto the field, the old women in the crowd would whack the opposing players with their umbrellas.'

Pagey got on well with the Wakefield coach, an affable bloke by the name of Ken Trail. While Dunc was trialling with the club, Ken sat the Aussie on the bench beside him and explained the English way of playing rugby league. The bench was on the sidelines under a small dugout or weather shelter. In the north of England each ground had its own peculiarities but the one constant was the touchlines were never far from the stands or the people sitting in them – 'maybe twenty feet or so away'. Dunc remembers one night particularly well. The game was in 'Uddersfield or Ull' – he isn't sure which, except that the name of the town started with the letter 'h'. During a lull in the game, Ken leaned over to his Aussie pupil and said, 'Eeeh lad, think it's time we livened things up'. He reached into his bag and pulled out an orange (probably intended for half time). Ken then stuck his head out of the security of the shed, yelled something rude and threw the orange into the crowd. He had a huge grin on his face when he sat back down and gave Dunc a knowing look. The Aussie newcomer wasn't entirely prepared for the crowd's reaction. An absolute fusillade of coals landed on the roof of the weathershed. It seems the local fans regarded it as a badge of honour to support their club by bringing coals to the game and hurling them at anyone who incurred their displeasure. Some of the projectiles bounced off the roof of the shed and struck the linesmen. The irate official promptly stooped down, picked up the coal and fired it right back at the offenders.

Pagey was a spectator at the ground when the Australian team played a game against Wakefield Trinity as a warm-up for a test match. The Aussies led by a point with a minute to go and the locals were baying for blood – antipodean blood at that. With a minute to go the referee found a penalty in Wakefield's favour. Neil Fox was an accurate kicker although his range was limited and the spot was close to his limit. The ref turned his back and Neil, seeing this, quickly pinched a yard or two. Not a peep from the crowd. He teed the ball up on a mound of sand and stepped back to take the kick toe-poke style. One, two, three steps and the ball arched toward the posts only to land a good two or three yards short. Didn't matter. The ref gave the goal and Wakefield left the field victorious. Pagey happened to know the referee, the local school master, and approached him for an explanation. 'Mate that kick was way short, so why did you allow it?' The response was quick, and in a thick Yorkshire voice it said, 'Aye lad, kick weren't right but listen to me. You Aussies, you're here for five minutes. Me? I've got to live here.' As for Neil Fox, he captained both Wakefield-Trinity and England and, despite those duties, he still managed to report for work 'down in pit eight hours a day'.

When he wasn't being assailed by lumps of coal and questioning dodgy referees, things were definitely on the up for Dunc. The Wakefield Trinity club looked forward to the contributions of their Aussie imports. The locals were confident the Challenge Cup was all but in the club's back pocket. But a fly in the ointment arrived to spoil their happy anticipation. It was bound to happen. Things were going too smoothly – something was just waiting to go wrong. And something did. At that time the Aussie and Pommie league bosses were at loggerheads. The dispute, you may not be surprised to learn, centred on money. There was a long-standing and nagging fiscal imbalance that weighed heavily in England's favour. The English Rugby League demanded and received a fifty per cent share of all gate takings when touring Australia. The Aussies, by contrast, pocketed only one third of takings when they toured England. Bill Buckley, the Australian league supremo, wasn't copping any more financial chicanery on the part of the rapacious Poms. He took immediate and forceful action, issuing an edict stating that no Australian player will be released to play in England until full financial parity was reached for touring teams. Anyone familiar with rugby league officials would naturally suspect that Bill's objections were expressed in far less diplomatic terms, but no one was in any doubt about what he was after. Among the Aussies caught in the cross hairs of this dispute were none other than Duncan Page and John Whelan, two potential first graders in a star-studded Wakefield Trinity side. Ah well, there's no helping bad luck – it wasn't going to be Wakefield for the disappointed boys. Johnny shot through while Dunc decided to hang around a bit longer. But after a while it was back to Oz for him too.

In no time he was happily ensconced in the comforts of his birthplace – the St George district. He wasn't worried. Something was bound to come up. It always did. Mum was cooking for him again and there were definitely no ghosts or graveyards in the vicinity of that happy Blakehurst home.

11

ST GEORGE BOY

With Modern Pentathlon still in the future, and with his recent English adventure behind him, Dunc thought he might take a shot at trialling for the St George Rugby League team. Even though there were many codes of football available to him it just had to be rugby league. In the Sydney of that era, anyone who questioned Dunc's decision would be considered completely stupid. Rugby league was Sydney's game. Shire against shire, suburb against suburb. Every kid growing up in the St George district followed the Dragons and harboured secret ambitions of wearing the red vee. The Saints ruled the roost during the fifties and sixties by winning eleven consecutive premierships. It was a big step even to consider winning a spot in a side populated by invincible demigods. All the same, the reception he received at Wakefield gave Pagey the appetite and confidence to test his skills against the best in Australia. Hadn't he done just that in England and cut the mustard? He might as well give the Dragons a go. Face it – he would still be in Wakefield sprinting to be first to the baths if Bill Buckley hadn't gone and stuffed things up!

Before the start of each season St George conducted annual trials for aspiring players. Sometimes over a hundred blokes showed up to vie for a spot in the fabled team – many signing their names as 'A. N. Other' or 'A. Nother'. The process was pretty straightforward – front up, run on the paddock and show the sharp-eyed men on the sidelines what you can do. They knew what they were looking for. Each wannabe had ten minutes to strut his stuff. After that, as Dunc laughingly remembers, 'There were two responses – it was either "don't bother coming back son", or "okay mate, see you next week".' Pagey's first outing went well; he scored a couple of tries and was invited back. The next week he scored a couple more. It was the same the following week and the week after that. All this, mind you, without mentioning a word to the men in the know that he had been signed by Wakefield Trinity. Sometimes the man's inherent modesty worked against him. At the end of the pre-season trials the culling was complete, and the only newcomer deemed good enough to wear the Dragons jumper in the coming 1961 season was the promising winger, Duncan McIntyre Page.

Over the years St George earned the reputation of being a well-run club. Its management scrupulously insisted that all formalities must be followed. The man in charge of the fine print was the formidable Frank Facer, the legendary major domo during the Saints' fabled run. Facer presided over the champions during their remarkable string of eleven consecutive premierships. All the players, even the all-time greats, were warily respectful of Mr Facer. As the only newbie that year, Dunc was called into the imposing man's office for a sit down. From across his desk, Facer gruffly asked, 'How much do you want son?' No niceties, no 'pleased to have you on board' or 'we expect big things from you this season'. No sweet talk from Frank Facer; the man was all business. Dunc said he thought the old bloke was going to fall off his chair when he answered, 'I don't want anything thank you Mr Facer'. Pagey thinks his response must have been a first because it completely frazzled the great Frank. 'I could tell by the look on his face he hadn't heard that before.' After pulling himself together, Facer demanded to know what the young whippersnapper was talking about. Unfazed by the intimidating supremo, Duncan explained that he still harboured Olympic ambitions and it was important to retain his amateur status. That was fine with the old boy – he was signing a promising player for less than peanuts. The chequebook slid back in its drawer. So Duncan Page signed on with St George as the only amateur among a club bedecked with seasoned and highly accomplished professionals.

The men on the sidelines, the kind who know about these things, were impressed with Duncan's blinding speed and his ability to sniff out a try. They concluded that he had earned his right to have a run on the wing. Dunc modestly concedes that, at one time, he did have exceptional speed over thirty metres. Certainly he was no slouch, because he had trained with the best sprinters NSW had to offer and beat them all out of the blocks. He thinks the only one to best him at the start was the Olympian Hec Hogan. 'That quickness stood me in good stead when I decided to play league.' The sprinter's burst must have helped a bit, one likes to think – the only newcomer graded in 1961 is solid evidence that somebody thought he was worth a chance.

It was only natural that the newcomer was selected for his first run on performance in second grade. The St George second grade side was a crash hot unit and, as general opinion had it, the Saints' seconds could beat most first grade sides. The night before his first game, Dunc eagerly scanned the newspapers until there, in black and white, he found his name. The game was a trial match against Western Suburbs, a team with a long history of brutal encounters against the Saints, including one extremely dubious grand final loss. Dunc checked out the West's side to find his opposing winger. He found it all right and nearly had a cardiac arrest. The pleasant glow that comes with achievement abruptly subsided when he saw the fatal words spelling out the dreaded name – 'Peter Dimond'. Pagey, the furthest thing from a swearing man, must have been tempted to let fly when he saw that. Fate decreed that he (along with John Riley on the other wing) was lined up against the fearsome Wests winger.

Some explanation for Dunc's consternation is in order. Peter Dimond came by his formidable reputation honestly. Whether playing against Sydney opponents or those from Great Britain, he dished out the rough stuff with no compunction. If he could give it, Dimond was also ready to take it, and he never backed down. The equally formidable English prop forward, Cliff Watson, when asked what he regarded as his toughest match against Australia, laughingly came up with an anecdote. At the time the question was asked, Cliffy had come out to Oz to have a run with the Cronulla-Sutherland side. It was 1973 and he and his Pommie mate, the infinitely annoying halfback Tommy Bishop, guided the Sharks to a grand final appearance against Manly. Cliff's words went something like, 'Hardest game I ever had were game I didn't play in. There I was, mindin' me own business in Wembley tunnel before test match, and that bugger Peter Dimond king hit me. I was out like a light.

Don't remember much of that game I can tell you.' It seems the volatile Peter Dimond couldn't wait to get out on the paddock to commence hostilities. Whether or not Cliffy's story is genuine or apocryphal, it reflects the temper of the times and the combative nature of Peter Dimond. He was the last bloke Pagey wanted to line up against in his first outing.

The good Lord must have been smiling on a Blakehurst bedroom on the morning of the game because, after a night of interrupted sleep, Duncan Page learned that the cause of his bad dreams had pulled out of the game with a nagging injury. The vastly relieved newcomer went on to do 'okay' in his first game wearing the red and white. In fact, all his early outings were 'okay'. Okay being three tries in the first match, two in the second and several more in the next two. After four games in second grade where he teamed up with future luminaries Billy Smith and fellow North Cronulla Beach Sprint relay member, John Riley, Dunc was called up to first grade. All up it was four games in seconds and then he was running on with the big boys. Years later John Riley and Dunc were having a cordial chat at some function and the former North Cronulla boys agreed that it was 'no disgrace' to have a run in second grade during St George's fabled era.

After his time with the champions in the Wakefield-Trinity side, the newcomer wasn't about to be overawed when he walked into the dressing sheds at Jubilee Oval or the Sydney Cricket Ground. The Saints usually featured on the 'game of the day' which was always played at the SCG, so the cricket ground was really a home away from home. Pagey couldn't help feeling slightly star struck when he was in close proximity to these legends of league. The names trip off the tongue – Provan, Raper, Ryan and Gasnier are but a few. Reg Gasnier was the big one for Pagey. Gaz, the Prince of Centres, was a work of art when in full flight. With the ball carried high on his chest and his head flung back, he appeared to float above the green sward of the SCG. Teammates, especially the wingers, knew that if they wanted to make themselves look good, all they had to do was 'stay close to Gaz'. Dunc's prime ambition was to play on the wing outside 'the Prince of Centres', and his second grade form made that dream increasingly likely.

Good luck was never a feature of his time at St George. A prime example came in his initial run in the first-grade side. He had been called up to replace the injured – wait for it – Reg Gasnier. Down the gurgler went another ambition and, as it eventuated, never to be realised. Not to worry, Dunc scored a try and performed reasonably well in his initial run in firsts. He went on to do the same the following week. After that, with Gaz restored to peak health, the newbie was dropped back to seconds. With that demotion, what had been such a bright beginning to Dunc's rugby league career was cruelly shattered by an unmitigated disaster. Rushing to tackle an opponent over the sideline, Pagey's sprigs got stuck in the turf. Then, in a lethal example of friendly fire, a teammate attempting to tackle the same opponent, crashed full into Pagey's leg. It was Dunc's dreadful mischance that his leg was still trapped by the sprigs of his boot. Not only did the injury look bad – it was bad. After being stretchered off, two trainee medical attendants determined that the leg was broken in six places. The subsequent treatment involved a prolonged series of medical decisions of dubious levels of competence. The incompetence started with his right leg being put in plaster on four different occasions. It stayed in its cast for six months. In truth the unsatisfactory medical treatment continued unabated. Dunc's leg was never repaired satisfactorily, and the injury continues to plague him to this very day.

Ever the optimist, Pagey blithely assumed that when the leg was mended, everything would get back to normal. Never has positive thinking been more misplaced. When the cast was finally removed, the patient discovered that his right foot, no longer slightly pigeon toed, was now on a distinct angle so that both feet pointed in the same direction. The 'recovery' was prolonged. During the process Dunc occupied himself by lifting weights. He chose to ignore the advice of those who claimed he would become 'muscle bound'. Seeing as how he had lifted weights since his time in the wilds of Moree, the bloke pumping the iron had a fair idea of what worked for him. But it was a long road – even to partial recovery. No compensation in any form came from St George and, as Dunc had given up his interest in the driving range before leaving for Jersey, the finances were a bit dicey. Yet again Jessie and Cy came to the rescue and generously chipped in until their adventurous boy was on his feet again – literally.

The leg eventually healed but it was never any good. His feet looked weird and he couldn't trust his bung leg. Things were crook. He couldn't come close to running like he was accustomed to. 'Look, I knew it was a bad injury, but I didn't think it was that bad. But it wasn't long before I realised I would never play football again.' A couple of weeks after he was out of plaster Pagey was at Hurstville Oval and immediately discovered how badly things had turned out. 'I knew straightaway that I was shot.' His 440 time was 30 seconds slower than what he was running pre-injury. He had a go at the hundred sprint and a bloke he used to beat by ten yards beat him by the same margin. His formerly superb biomechanics were totally out of whack. The man who set, and still retains, the record for the 100-yard sprint at Jubilee Oval was a shadow of what he had been. His time of 9.8 seconds on grass will never be equalled. Why? Because the ground has been altered to meet the needs of rugby league. Pagey's record will never be bettered.

Perhaps the most impressive thing about Duncan Page is the attitude he brings when forced to confront adversity. Somehow, after shattering a leg and having to accept the demise of a promising rugby league career, Pagey found room for a positive outlook. Misfortunes that would have reduced others to tears were overcome by sheer fortitude. He remembers one day, while staring into a Kogarah shop window, one of the many doctors who had tried to repair his leg recognised him and stopped for a chat. In the course of their conversation, the good doctor admitted that he had made a mistake when operating on Dunc's leg and wished he had done things differently. Pagey is never one to play the blame game and is philosophical about the bungled response to his most severe injury. 'Look, it was a bad break and it was badly managed, but that's just how things were. There was no such thing as sports medicine in those days. You had to have faith in the doctors and hope that things worked for the best.'

UNSTOPPABLE

As it happened, things didn't work out at St George but, in the aftermath of that crushing experience, nothing was going to stop him from following the light he saw shining in the darkness. It was time for Modern Pentathlon to stand front and centre in his sporting ambitions. An inconsequential injury wasn't going to deter him from pursuing his dream.

12

ANOTHER DOOR OPENS

In the end Dunc underwent six separate operations but nothing worked. The leg never set properly and finally the ankle froze; it had almost no flexibility. In his own words it was a 'complete catastrophe'. Month after long month went past and yet he still clung to the hope that the leg would heal. After what the poor bloke had been through, no one would have blamed him if he curled up under his blankie, stuck a thumb in his mouth and had a good old sook. But self-pity has never been part of Pagey's modus operandi. A buggered leg wasn't going to put an end to his Olympic goal. True, the glory days of the beach sprint and the early promise at Wakefield Trinity and St George were consigned to yesterday's sports pages. Even surfing was nearly impossible – with a frozen ankle he was able to stand on his board but there was no way he could balance properly. In the midst of all the gloom a chink of light shone through a partially opened door. And, when it was fully opened, the light revealed a new career in Modern Pentathlon. On one leg Duncan McIntyre Page quite literally hopped out of life as a local sporting hero into the world of international and Olympic competition.

Pagey's unstoppable ambition to represent his country at the Olympics had never wavered – not even during the dark days of his unsuccessful recuperation. The brutal reality of his situation sank in and he had to face the facts – never again would he be a 400-metre hurdler or a half miler. The lame duck changed direction to follow the beacon of Modern Pentathlon which guided him along a path to unimagined adventure. Once, in a quiet moment of reflection on his sporting hits and misses, Dunc acknowledged the guiding hand of destiny. 'I've never told anyone this, but for every setback another door always seemed to open for me. Something always just turned up.' And this time it was pentathlon that turned up. It was spurred on by the extravagant tales of Terry Nicoll and the taste of Modern Pentathlon down at Lang Lang.

After that early exposure it was a no-brainer – he knew he had to have a go at pentathlon. Hampered by a mangled leg, he knew he was spotting the others a big start, but his strengths in riding and shooting gave him confidence that he could improve his swimming and fencing along the way. Running? He would just have to make do. Pagey's Olympic dream never faltered – he may not be the leading member of the team, but at least he would be a part of it.

A career in rugby league may have snapped like a twig, but another shot at the Olympics – this time in Modern Pentathlon – sent up promising green shoots. 'So, what else was I going to do? I had to do something.' Dunc's interest in pentathlon received further encouragement from his developing friendship with Peter Macken. He had come to know Pete during the long months of his incapacitation and 'liked him'. So with a bit of help from his friends, he walked through the door that opened on a new phase of his sporting career.

The military origin of Modern Pentathlon is impossible to avoid. Indeed, one of its more prominent early exponents was none other than 'Old Blood and Guts' himself – that's right, the famous or infamous, depending on your perspective, General George Patton represented the United States in the 1912 Olympics at Stockholm. The competition, as the General and Pagey would be well aware, was far different from what it has become today. In their era it was held over five consecutive days and proved a severe test of the competitors' abilities and staying power. Today the competition has been reduced to fit the time frame of a single day. No doubt the old boys would scoff at its present shortened form but that is just a sign of the times. Oldies everywhere grumble that everything and everyone is in a rush these days. Modern Pentathlon isn't immune and has had to meet the demands of the times.

When you consider the order of the pentathlon events in competition, the martial tone becomes strikingly obvious. Indeed, in Duncan's day, a majority of the competitors were drawn from the armed services of various countries. Most overseas competitors were members of one of the military forces. Not for Pete, Dunc and Don though – they were thoroughly civilian Aussies. Whatever the occupational status of the competitors, the event was not for the faint-hearted. It was a stern test of stamina and courage; especially when it came to the ride. If you survived the equestrian course on the first day, there were still four days remaining and each presented its own set of unique difficulties.

Up to fifty competitors assembled to start things off. First event on the agenda was a cross-country ride over five thousand metres and usually containing twenty-five jumps of varying difficulty. The ride represented a soldier being given a message and then ordered to deliver it until his horse failed or was shot out from under him. Next came the fencing event. Here the unhorsed soldier is expected to fight his way through imaginary enemy lines and deliver the message. The fencing competitors used the épée – a thrusting weapon – that required one hit on an opponent to claim victory. There could be as many as fifty contests and each athlete was required to fence every one of the others. Next came the pistol shoot where competitors are allowed a five shot warm up and then four sequences of five shots are tallied until a final score is obtained. In all, competitors fired a total of twenty shots at a turning silhouette (human) target which represents the imaginary soldier shooting his way out of imaginary trouble. Once the bullets stop flying, the competitors head to the pool and are required to swim 300 metres. Points are allocated on the basis of the individual time each swimmer records. This event represents the valiant soldier, still carrying the message, swimming across an imaginary river. When he has dragged himself up the banks of the imaginary watercourse, his final duty is to undertake a cross country run of 4,000 metres – at the end of which the exhausted soldier successfully delivers the imaginary message.

At an Olympic event, success in Modern Pentathlon was based on the culmination of five days of intense competition. Each competitor was graded on his performance in each of the five events and the points were then tallied upon completion. Once the points are tabulated, the individual medallists were determined. Individual success is commendable, but Modern Pentathlon is first and foremost a team sport with the combined totals for each country's athletes determining the winning nation and each subsequent nation's standing. No matter how things go on a particular day, individual competitors bust a gut to perform to the best of their ability. This was certainly the case when Page, Macken and McMiken wore the green and gold. They had made too many sacrifices just to get there – pride in themselves and their country meant that they never gave anything less than their best shot.

As for Dunc's individual performances, he is always brutally honest when asked to rate himself in the five events. In two of them, the ride and the shoot, he was a complete natural. It was the others – fencing, swimming and the run – that were particular challenges. Over time he showed considerable improvement in the fence and the swim, but the run . . . oh dear, the run . . . performing at his earlier standard was beyond him. In what is probably the greatest irony of his life, the man selected for the '56 Olympic train-on squad with an eye squarely on his future as a runner, now quite literally dragged himself around the cross-country course. Never once will you hear him complain about his infirmity but, when pushed on the subject, he grudgingly concedes, 'I would have done a lot better if I could have run like I used to'.

Duncan Page is nothing if not the most modest of men. He constantly admonishes, 'Don't go making me look better than I was. Don't go talking me up.' He often prefaces his remarks, when relating an anecdote about his performance on some particular occasion, 'Now I don't want to go pumping up my tyres . . .' It was an understated but nothing less than candid Pagey who, when asked to rate his performance in the various pentathlon events, started with the ride. 'Always perilous' was how he described it. Competitors drew the number of their horse from a hat and, knowing nothing about their mount's ability, were expected to guide it around the cross-country course over jumps and through water until they came to the finish. At best the ride was a dicey proposition because it involved completing a dangerous course on an unknown horse. No wonder Dunc described it as 'perilous'. But the ride was one of his strengths and, as he reluctantly admitted, 'I think I was a good rider'. That self-assessment seems bang on the money. When he later wound up at Fort Sam in Texas, Colonel John Russell, the crusty old riding instructor, often used Pagey to demonstrate the correct technique for taking a horse over the jumps. For some reason, Pagey was undaunted by the ride. 'I was never nervous before the ride. It didn't seem to faze me.'

With riding ticked off as a positive, Pagey moved on to fencing and out came the candour – 'early on I was not much chop'. After a lot of work and, with the passage of time, he concedes, 'I got better'. By international standards Dunc rated himself as only a 'fair' fencer but things were different at home. By Australian standards he was making great strides. So much so that by 1966 he finished third in the Australian fencing championships. Then at Mexico in 1968 he and Peter finished numbers one and two in Australian fencing team results. How did they do that? Easy. In addition to their pentathlon duties, they were selected in the Australian épée team. Dunc surprised himself by finishing first among all Australian competitors. And that's where Mr Inherently Modest re-enters the picture. 'Even though I beat him in fencing at times, I always reckoned Peter was a better fencer than me.' Better or not (and they can sort that out for themselves), by sheer hard work and persistence Dunc made what started out as a liability – his fencing performance – into a pentathlon asset.

The shoot came next. It wasn't exactly 'pistols at dawn' but it was equally nerve-racking. The firearm of choice for Pete and Dunc was a Smith and Wesson K22 while Don preferred a Hammerli 22. The .22 calibre had less recoil after firing and that allowed them a quicker sight on the next target. As the targets steadily appeared, Pagey used a version of a Zen chant – 'align the sights and squeeze the trigger'. It must have worked because between them, the three Aussies became the best pentathlon shooting team in the world 'all up'. 'In every major competition as a team we either won the comp or individually.' The results were there for all to see: two second placings in World Pentathlon Championships and in all competitions they shot Australian records three times. In fact, they regularly outperformed those who had been selected for the Australian pistol team. When questioned why they hadn't put up their hands for selection in the Aussie pistol team, the reply is matter of fact: 'It never entered our minds to contest the pistol shoot.' Head to head, he shared pistol shooting honours with Pete although Dunc is quick to say that his great mate shot the highest score by two points. Ah well, what's two points between friends? Given that the shoot was such a strong Page asset, it is now clear that the experience of hypothermia in Vancouver and pinging vermin at Moree contributed to his pentathlon prowess.

Now we head over to the pool for the swim. Duke Kahanamoku established the precedent for surfers becoming Olympic swimmers and Pagey followed in his wake, both on a board and in the pool. Asked about his swimming ability, he says he had to 'rate myself as just ordinary'. The problem was obvious. 'I couldn't swim effectively because I couldn't kick.' The frozen ankle didn't allow the flexibility needed to develop an efficient kick. Even with that component absent, he persisted and gradually improved his times. Dunc generously concedes that serious improvement didn't eventuate until he came under the tutelage of Terry Gathercole, later the coach of the Australian swim team. While they were at Fort Sam, Pete and Dunc were forced to set their own swim training schedules after realising that the American swim coach had nothing to offer them. The 'coach' assigned to supervise the swimmers was a portly gentleman who showed up each day and ensconced himself under the shade of an umbrella. He thereupon set out to smoke about twenty cigarettes while slowly perusing the newspaper. It didn't take long before the boys realised there was no help coming from him. As Dunc tartly observed: 'Why would you take any notice of a fat guy sitting under a beach umbrella? What were we going to learn from him?'

With his performance in the swim a lot less than a positive asset, we now come to a decided liability – the run. When asked about that event, Dunc is unsparing and lets it all hang out: 'I rated myself as hopeless'. Nevertheless he dragged himself around the 4,000 metre cross-country course as best he could. If effort was required, then effort would be given. One brief anecdote is sufficient to demonstrate the extent of his struggles in the run. There was an Olympic trial held at Sydney's Centennial Park. Pagey, who was determined to make the team, left nothing behind on the course. 'I was often completely spent at the end of the run and didn't have the energy to stay on my feet. Sometimes at the finish I just couldn't stand so I fell on my hands and knees.' On this particular day, after an impressive end-of-run nosedive, the spectators were duly sympathetic – with one exception. That exception was none other than Terry Nicoll, the bloke with the inflated opinion of his abilities. At the sight of the exhausted Pagey, the ever-loquacious Terry couldn't help himself. He just had to air his considered opinion; the temptation was too strong. Seeing Dunc's exhausted finish, he vented forth with his considered judgement, 'Ah he's just bunging it on'. Another Terry who happened to be standing nearby – Terry Gathercole – heard Nicoll's snide opinion and drily observed, 'He's not bunging it on mate, and anyway he's going to the Olympics and you're not!' When the selectors made their call, Dunc was on the plane with Pete and Don while Terry Nicoll stayed home sharing his tall tales with anyone who cared to listen.

13

REMEMBERING THE ALAMO

A lasting benefit that came with Dunc's whole-hearted commitment to Modern Pentathlon was the blessing of lifelong friendships, and one of them is Peter Macken, the quintessential pentathlete. His great mates Don McMiken and Pagey may dispute the 'quintessential' description, but Peter went to more Olympics than they did and that's just how it is. As testament to the bond that developed between the two men during that period of their lives, more than once Dunc has said: 'In all the ten or so years we were together I can't think of a single time when we had an argument or a serious disagreement.' That stands as testament to their unity of purpose and dedication to the team's success. The Australian Modern Pentathlon team of that era was exceptional for its determination to achieve its best for the green and gold. The boys would bust a gut to achieve individual success but the team result was always their prime focus. In another lifetime they would have linked arms to repeat the musketeers' resounding cry of 'One for all and all for one'.

Modern Pentathlon has always been the ugly duckling of Olympic competition and suffered chronic neglect because it never gained the status of being a big-ticket event. It was always on the periphery of the glamour competitions like swimming and, during the fifties and sixties at least, athletics. Australian pentathletes, if given any exposure at all, found that they were relegated to the nether world of the sports pages alongside the race results. The stark reality for pentathlon was that it received little attention and even less financial support from the powers that be. If you wanted to take up Modern Pentathlon you had to be prepared to dig deep into your own back pocket. And if you wanted to compete at the highest level you had to forgo several years of career and a steady income. Without the kind of support the high profile sports received, it boiled down to this: if you wanted to improve as a pentathlete, it was imperative to look overseas. So when Australian Army

Major Wilbur Wright, an official in the NSW Modern Pentathlon association, was contacted by his American counterpart with an offer to base two Australian athletes at Fort Sam in Texas, the word immediately went out. It was a great offer – room and board with access to world class pentathlon training facilities and coaches.

Peter Macken, the established performer on the team, considered the offer for about ten seconds and said, 'Count me in'. Dunc, who at the time was merely an aspirant, also put up his hand. 'I didn't have to think twice. I knew I wasn't going to be playing football because of my crook leg, so I told Peter, "I'm with you. They can count me in too." It was that simple.' The boys packed their bags and were off to Fort Sam Houston in San Antonio, Texas – Fort Sam and San Antone as they are colloquially known. It was too good an offer for a broken-down former rugby league player to refuse. In his wildest dreams he would never expect to be given the opportunity to train at an army base in south Texas, but that's exactly where he was headed. It was 1962 and by then Pagey was totally committed to Modern Pentathlon. One way or another, he was determined to chase down his dream – the dream of wearing the green and gold. Despite the many obstacles he encountered along the way he never lost sight of his goal: 'It was always my ambition to make the Olympic team.' The out-of-the blue opportunity to train at Fort Sam was a once in a lifetime opportunity.

The boys set off for the States by ship and disembarked at Los Angeles. Peter got in touch with an American mate who had lived near him in Sydney and only recently returned to the States. Pete's mate drove a taxi in LA and he took great delight showing the boys the sights – Hollywood Boulevard with its walk of fame, Sunset Strip, which had a popular television show named after it. Of course, there was an obligatory visit to a strip club. Although Pagey recalls that there was a boxing match on the telly – a world welterweight championship bout between Emile Griffith and Benny 'Kid' Paret (who died during the bout) – so all eyes were focused on the boxers rather than the gyrating ladies. With the high life and bright lights of Hollywood behind them, the two Aussies boarded a Greyhound Bus to their next destination.

Fort Sam Houston is a major US Army base located outside San Antonio, just a stone's throw from the Alamo. The Alamo? The very place where Davy Crockett fought the Mexican Army to a standstill only to be overcome by insuperable odds. Yes sir that's it, the Alamo – the small Spanish mission so redolent of romantic American western legend. It is the site of the brave resistance of the Texans against the forces of General Santa Ana during the War of Independence. The fact that Davy, the fabled frontiersman, died in the carnage only adds to its mystique. To this day the cry of 'Remember the Alamo' is capable of stirring Texan blood. In a subsequent battle, it was the rallying cry of an outnumbered Texan force which fought and defeated the Mexican army and, in the aftermath, proudly captured Santa Ana himself. The exhortation to 'Remember the Alamo' may well have been the motivation that stirred up a group of Mexicans the day the boys arrived at Fort Sam and started to unpack their belongings.

Pete and Dunc's new home was the Bachelor Officers' Quarters at Fort Sam. It was a gracious old building that dated back to 1875. General Douglas MacArthur shared these same quarters during his time as a student there. Another noted figure whose presence graced the confines of Fort Sam was the legendary and terrifying Apache warrior, Geronimo. Dunc thinks it is highly unlikely that the rebellious Geronimo would have been offered the calibre of hospitality he and Peter received. The venerable two storey building was exclusively reserved for occupation by American pentathletes drawn from various branches of the US military forces – the recent arrivals being the only civilian exceptions.

Dunc was now nothing less than a seasoned world traveller when he tossed bags on the bed and decided to amble off to see the sights of San Antone. It was mid-afternoon and the March sun wasn't too taxing as he poked around the local supermarket. Large supermarkets catering for every possible whim of every possible customer were common in the States but were completely unknown in Australia. Pagey was fascinated: 'I had never seen a shop that big in my life, so I took the time to have a good look around'. An hour or so later, his consumer curiosity quelled, he returned to Fort Sam and tapped on Peter's door to tell him about his discovery. 'Who's there?' The returning shopper was unamused. 'It's me, who do you think it is? Who else do you know here?' The door opened quickly and with peremptory haste Pagey was hauled into the room. Pete quickly checked out the hallway before slamming the door. The reason for the unexpected urgency was pretty obvious once Peter calmed down. As he explained the situation, while Dunc was amusing himself in the shopping centre, a murder had been committed little more than fifty yards from their quarters. The military police came knocking in search of the guilty party – rudely interrupting Pete's nap. They questioned him at length, no doubt trying to decode the strange accent in the process. The MPs wanted to know who he was and what he was doing there. Satisfied with the explanation, they advised him to lock himself in his room and then left him to his own devices. So there Pete lingered, in a strange room a long way from home, waiting for the killer to return and claim another victim. Remember one important thing – Peter Macken and Duncan Page were nothing less than crack shots. They had immediate access to firearms and they knew how to use them – their pistols were always within easy reach. After hearing Pete's tale, Dunc loaded up and sat on the bed with pistol in hand waiting for the murderer to show himself. Peter laughs out loud when recounting his version of events. 'Dunc sat there on the bed with his pistol and I reckon he would have blasted the first person to touch that door handle.' Just another ordinary day in Texas.

In the end the bad guy didn't show up but there was to be more fun and games that night. After sundown the boys heard the unmistakable sounds of a raging gun battle not too far away from their quarters. They kept their heads down and tried for sleep only to be informed the next morning that a large group of Mexicans and the police had been involved in a good old-fashioned frontier shootout. There may be some historical significance to the affray. Pagey recalls that they arrived at Fort Sam sometime in early March but is hazy on the exact date. Peter's memory is no help either. It may be a matter of coincidence, but the Battle of the Alamo ended on March 6, 1836. Might not the boys have stumbled across a Mexican desire to re-enact their historic Alamo victory only to be vanquished, a century or so later, by the forces of truth, justice and the Texas way? Whatever prompted the dispute, the Aussies were treated to a rip-snorter of a Texas welcome at Fort Sam. Dunc still speaks in wonder about their first day on the base and concedes that he probably should have expected nothing less. On the way there he spotted one branch of the constabulary (he thinks it was the Highway Patrol) proudly sporting Texans longhorns on the hoods (bonnets) of their cars. The boys from Down Under had been given a proper Wild West welcome – from then on it was 'Howdy partners' all around.

They hadn't come all that way to hide in their rooms, so the very next morning they started training. When asked about his initial impressions of Fort Sam: 'I didn't have time to think about anything, they put us to work straight away'. Flat chat was the order of the first day of training. The regime at Fort Sam never varied; the pentathletes started off each day with a ride under the eagle-eyed supervision of Colonel John Russell, US Army. Both Peter and Dunc speak of the man with considerable respect. Dunc particularly recalls meeting the man that first morning: 'He was in his office with a cup of coffee and chomping on a big cigar'. Crusty old soldier that he was, John Russell may sound like someone from central casting, but Pagey is adamant that he was a first-rate teacher. The riding courses the Colonel devised were so rigorous and challenging that when his charges encountered other cross-country competition venues, they were well prepared. 'Once you'd ridden around the courses at Fort Sam, the other courses in the world didn't seem so bad.' During their morning rides Colonel Russell drove the boys hard and lectured them endlessly on the correct way to do things. Dunc remembers him insisting that 'you must approach the jumps correctly and give your horse every opportunity to succeed'. Some of his students listened attentively and took his word as gospel, some must have been daydreaming, because Pagey has pictures of falls which are nothing less than spectacular. When asked whether the ride was the most dangerous of all the events, Duncan replies, 'Well, it was certainly the most dramatic'.

Fortunately for Pagey, he was a quick learner and the kind of student who put theory into practice. Colonel Russell often used him to demonstrate correct techniques to the others. A relationship of sorts developed between teacher and pupil as is evident when Duncan first encountered 'The Slide'. A much dreaded obstacle on one of Fort Sam's many riding courses, The Slide was just that – a twenty foot high, nearly vertical slide that ended up two hundred yards short of Salado Creek, a watercourse that ran past Fort Sam. Pagey recalls the day when the Colonel and he rode along the creek until they came upon The Slide. Dunc pulled up his horse and peered over the edge of the sheer drop. 'What goes down there?' he asked. His instructor took the cigar from his mouth and gave the questioner one of his flinty-eyed looks. He coyly measured the steep drop and, after a long pause, his reply was terse and to the point. In true military style the old warrior said, 'Tomorrow, Dunc you do'.

Tomorrow came soon enough and as promised, so did The Slide. On his first attempt to negotiate its precipitate slope, the inevitable happened. Pagey did what he could to stay on his mount but horse and rider parted company. Dunc slid up and off the horse's neck in what felt like slow motion. Rider and horse wound up in Salado Creek with Dunc flat on his back and the horse walking over him. Neither party was injured so Pagey remounted and rode back to join the group of spectators who were thoroughly enjoying themselves at his expense. Without a trace of sympathy, the Colonel addressed the soaked rider and gave him step-by-step instructions on the correct way to approach the slide. Dunc must have listened attentively because he never came off on that particular obstacle again. Today he can chuckle when he recalls that 'a lot of the others weren't so lucky'. At times he speaks reflectively about his experiences on the Fort Sam cross-country courses saying that it 'brought a lot of fellows undone'. From the acute perspective of hindsight he can speak objectively about the benefits of the gruelling experiences at his home course, 'When we would walk a course the night before an event, a lot of the competitors were very apprehensive. If I hadn't trained at Fort Sam, and it was the first time I saw some of those courses, I would have said, "Stagger me!"' He followed that with a deep laugh. Duncan Page is never one to resort to profanity.

The flinty old colonel was a hard taskmaster, but he knew what he was talking about. He had been there and done that. You aren't appointed captain of the US equestrian team without good reason. Exacting martinet that he was, he was occasionally capable of punctuating his curtness with flashes of sardonic humour. He always started the day's ride by instructing his men to go out there and 'find a horse you think you can ride'. Well, one day Dunc thought he could ride a horse called 'Eight Ball'. He had never ridden him before but in time he got to know the horse well. 'I liked Eight Ball. He was always a quirky horse who liked to pull to the left as you approached a jump. Very few riders completed a course with him.'

Colonel Russell liked to vary the training routine by designing shorter rides which he used as time trials. It was a way of reminding his students of the demands of the unforgiving minute. On one of those trials, and with a left leaning horse, Pagey set off on the course. Things went well until he and Eight Ball came to a fork in the track. Horse wanted to go left; rider attempted to guide him to the right. The result was a compromise. Horse and rider crashed into the large tree that stood in the middle of both tracks. 'I'd never ridden Eight Ball before that day, so we wound up going straight ahead until I was wiped out by that big old tree.' Eight Ball shot through while Dunc picked himself up and walked back in. And who was waiting for him, stopwatch in hand? None other than the cigar chomping Colonel. The stony-faced mentor looked at the straggler, checked his watch and wryly said, 'Dunc we usually finish the course in seven and a half minutes. It took you half an hour and you finished on foot'. Pagey remembers the incident with glee today and he bears no ill will to the recalcitrant Eight Ball – putting it all down to the vagaries of chance.

The pentathlon ride, probably because of its risk to life and limb, takes pride of place when Dunc reminisces about his days with Pete and Don. But the program at Fort Sam also provided them with high quality coaching that was absent in some of the other disciplines. The swimming coach has been done and dealt with earlier, but Pagey has fond memories of the pool which was 'a beautiful place to swim'. It was built around a natural spring that had been made into an Olympic length pool with wooden turning boards at each end. One of the pool's chief assets was its location. It was situated just behind the Lone Star Brewery; a favourite watering hole for the pentathletes.

The fencing coach was another thing altogether. He was a Frenchman who flatly refused to coach anyone who wasn't prepared to do things his way. His dogmatic insistence boiled down to one iron-clad demand: the preferred grip he insisted the fencers use with their épées. He was an ardent advocate of the French grip but at Fort Sam most of the pentathletes preferred the pistol grip. The arcane matter of fencing grips is far too abstruse to elaborate here, but the upshot was that the majority of Fort Sam's fencers opted to train among themselves rather than use a grip they found awkward and uncomfortable. A few converted to the Francophone way, but Peter and Dunc were not among them. In the end the Aussies didn't do too badly because their fencing accomplishments speak for themselves. When it came to the cross-country run, it was much the same – little or no coaching. Dunc remembers that the boys were 'left to our own devices'. It wasn't until much later, when they teamed up with Al Lawrence and Keith Ollerenshaw, that the Aussie pentathletes found running coaches who knew what they were talking about.

That left the shoot. The pistol coach was a colourful former boxer named George Murley. Dunc speaks of him with much fondness. It was he who gave the boys their mantra, 'align the sights and squeeze the trigger'. He accompanied that piece of wisdom with the warning: 'Believe me boys, between sighting and squeezing a terrible lot can happen'. If you were an all right sort of guy, George Murley was the kind of man who would give you the shirt off his back. He must have taken a shine to Pete and Dunc because he allowed them unrestricted use of his Cadillac during their stay at Fort

Sam. While his students cruised in style, George was happy to tootle around town in a VW Beetle. At the time, a Cadillac was the prime status symbol among American cars. The downside? They were notorious gas guzzlers. But Texas was the home of the oil business and Pagey laughs when he says that they didn't have to worry about going broke – not when petrol went for the exorbitant price of 14 cents a gallon (there are about four and a half litres in a gallon). George Murley and his wife enjoyed entertaining the pentathlon boys at their good ole Texas barbeques where they put on a magnificent spread. The Aussies were invited, arrived on time and were welcomed with genuine hospitality. As soon as he walked through the door Dunc was surprised to learn they were required to take off their jackets and shoes. The reason for this strange house rule? George was making it difficult for those who wanted to sneak away early.

It was never a wise move to try to slip away before the festivities ended – not just because their host wasn't keen on early leavers but because his wife might have taken it the wrong way. There had been a string of break-ins in the neighbourhood recently and one night the alert Mrs Murley witnessed a burglary in progress at the house next door. Like any good ole Texas lady would do, she reached for her pistol – a Colt 45 – and promptly let fly a couple of rounds at the intruder. She must have had a good pistol coach because one of her shots collected the wannabe burglar in the thigh. Dunc pauses in his recollection to observe: 'If anyone did that here, he would be put in the slammer. But not over there, she was given a citation and made a deputy sheriff of Bexar County' (Pronounced 'Bear', the county that incorporates San Antone and Fort Sam). Dunc shakes his head and goes on to say, 'Only in Texas'.

To round off his introduction to Fort Sam, Pagey recalls that after they had been in training for a few weeks a group of Mexican bandidos took it upon themselves to raid the PX (Post Exchange – a shop that is exclusive to the military). The robbers grabbed everything they could get their hands on and sprinted about five hundred yards across the parade ground where they took refuge in a small house nearby. Dunc watched from a safe distance while the

Military Police dealt with the matter by firing volleys of shots at the house. The fusillade continued for some time. The fracas ended, Pagey remembers, when a bedsheet was waved tentatively outside a window. Hostilities ceased and the culprits were apprehended.

After being a first-hand witness to the great PX robbery, Dunc took drastic action. 'One of the first things I did was to go down to a bargain basement store and buy myself a Smith and Wesson K38 Combat Masterpiece revolver.' There is no mention of ever needing to use the firearm.

For the boys from Oz, life at Fort Sam had certainly started off with a bang.

Cy and Jessie 1940, 'Mum wouldn't go to town without hat and gloves'.

Duncan and Clem Junior shaping up in the front yard at Blakehurst, 1946.

12-year-old Duncan on Big Red, 'like a prize ponce', 1946.

Battalion boxer, National Service.

Duncan, winning City vs Country hurdles for St George Amateur Athletics Club, 1954.

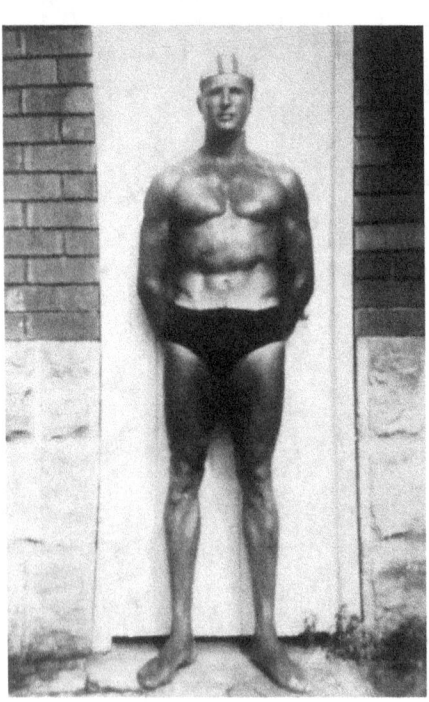

North Cronulla, 1959.   St George Boy, 1961.

Jersey lifesavers, Duncan in the middle, 1960.

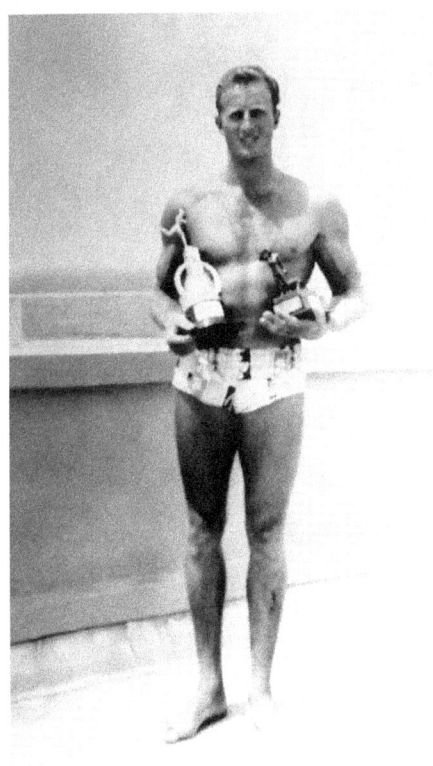

Duncan at North Cronulla Surf Lifesaving Club.

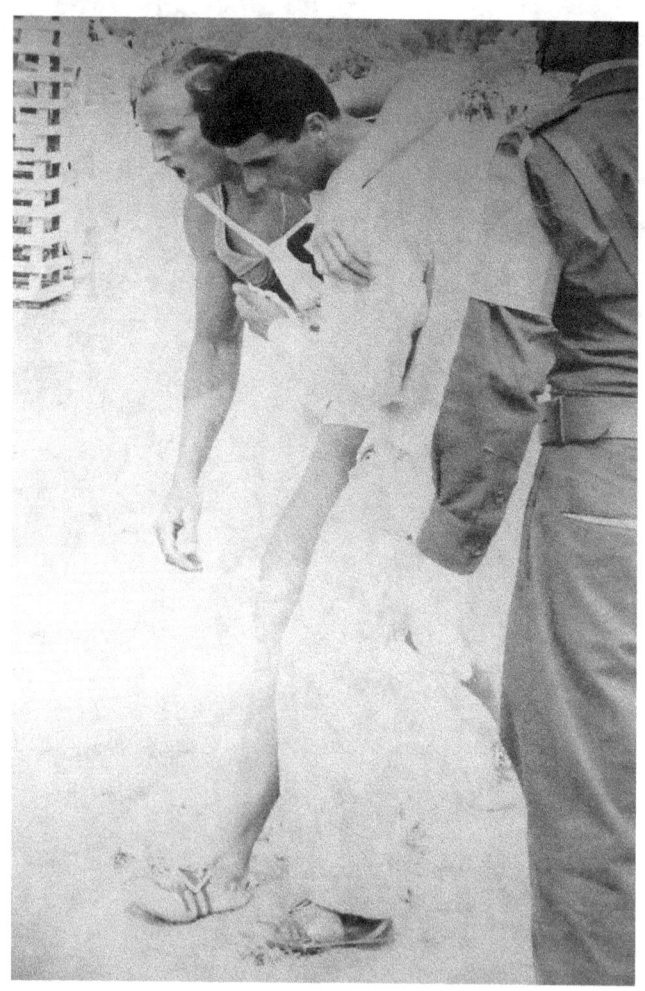

Duncan doing what it takes.

Training for Japan 1964, Terry Gathercole stopwatch in hand with the Pentathlon Three – Don McMiken, Duncan Page, Peter Macken.

Walking the course, Japan 1964 – Peter, Don, Japanese officer, Duncan and Lloyd Mitchelson (reserve).

Winner of the May Comp ride at Fort Sam, 1962. Duncan in a borrowed slouch hat.

At Duncan's house, 1980s. From left – Nev Seyers, Dunc, Peter Macken, Don McMiken and Terry Nicholl.

Australian Masters Powerlifting Championships, Brisbane, 1986.

Sydney 2000, carrying the torch.

14

'THE BEST YEAR OF MY LIFE'

It was hot as during the summer of '62 – 'stinking hot' is Pagey's memory. Texas summers are always like that. The bachelor quarters were 'as hot as hell in the nights', he says. Along with the heat came that summer's hottest music. Every time you turned on the radio, there was Ray Charles' 'I Can't Stop Loving You'. Dunc fondly remembers hearing Ray on the radio while he tossed and turned sleeplessly during those long Texas nights. 'They would play a different song and then on would come Ray again. Everywhere you went you heard that song.' Even today, hearing that song brings a smile. One familiar song is all it takes for the memories to come flooding back. 'It was the best year of my life.' That song and that summer are 'imprinted on my mind forever'.

Pete and Dunc's time at Fort Sam wasn't all about training. One doesn't have to possess an overly vivid imagination to picture what two Aussies blokes with the unfettered use of a Cadillac could get up to. The day they cruised down to Corpus Christie near the Gulf of Mexico was a prime example of their youthful shenanigans. It was an easy day's outing. Nothing arduous – just a mere 130 miles south of San Antone. The Caddie smoothed out the miles as if they were nothing. At 14 cents a gallon the boys weren't concerned about filling its gigantic gas tank. After a day's sightseeing and cavorting on a nearby beach, they found a safe spot on a flat stretch of sand where, at sundown, they bunked down for the night. Their choice of accommodation? The car of course. A Cadillac's seats, front and back, were as large (if not bigger) than your average Fort Sam bed. As a plan it seemed fine until, at some time in the night, Duncan rose to answer nature's call. He opened the Caddie's door and found that he was standing in water up to his ankles. Dunc jumped back in, woke Peter and they gunned George Murley's prized vehicle to the safety of higher ground.

'THE BEST YEAR OF MY LIFE'

You would have thought that after seeing the tide roll in and out in Jersey, Pagey might have had some inkling of how the ocean works. Apparently not. A further question arises from their sleeping arrangements. One might legitimately inquire – why sleep in the car in the first place? The answer is simple. These were Australian pentathletes who were always broke – there wasn't any money for extravagances like cheap motel rooms. They often had to dig deep just to feed themselves. After nearly drowning George Murley's Cadillac they pointed its long hood (bonnet) in the direction of San Antone and, as always, it delivered them safe and sound. Peter and Duncan were well looked after at the base and, for the remainder of that year, life was pretty sweet. Again, it is instructive to listen to Pagey, 'we couldn't have made it if it wasn't for Fort Sam'.

There was time for fun and games, but work was the number one priority. It always had the upper hand and that didn't allow much room for adventure. But when the opportunity arose, they seized it with both hands. There was the time they drove down to the University of Houston to catch up with Allan Lawrence who was there on an athletic scholarship. Al was a star member of the university track team along with Laurie Elliot, Herb's brother, and Pat Clohessy who later went on to train Robert De Castella among numerous others. The Aussies had a good old catch up and agreed to get together at the track meet at the university's stadium later in the day. Pete and Dunc went off to do the tourist bit and when they returned the irrepressible Al was ready and waiting. As soon as he spotted the boys making their entrance, he gave the ground announcer the nod. Al took the microphone and grandly announced his mates' arrival. His voice boomed out over a packed and attentive audience. 'Ladies and gentlemen put your hands together and give a good old Texas welcome to two Australian poofters who are visiting Houston. Stand up and take a bow Duncan Page and Peter Macken.'

Back then not a soul in the crowd, except a vagabond Aussie, would have a clue what Al was talking about. There was polite applause all around accompanied by friendly slaps on the backs of two profoundly embarrassed visitors. It never seemed to matter what Al said. He was the kind of bloke who could get away with anything. After all, with his outstanding performances on the track – not to mention his winning personality – he went on to become a favourite Houston son. As for Pete and Dunc's embarrassment, neither man has anything against people of that persuasion, but it would be harder to find two straighter than straight heteros. But that was never going to stop Al from taking the piss. So two beet-red and thoroughly mortified 'poofters' took their seats, pulled their heads in and accepted the acknowledgement of the crowd. Dunc still laughs at the memory and is grateful 'that back in those days no one in the States had any idea what the word meant. But that was Al Lawrence; you never knew what he was going to get up to next.'

Cadillacs and old friends made a welcome diversion from the incessant grind of training. 'We flogged ourselves every day'. There was no let up – they trained in all five sports each day and pushed themselves as hard as their bodies allowed. They operated on the misguided belief, prevalent at the time, that effort and effort alone improved performance. 'We thought that the harder you trained the better you went. Now I can see that we were always in a state of exhaustion.' Years later, they understood the error of their ways when they spoke to the Russian and Hungarian pentathletes at one of several world championships. 'We found out from them that they didn't do everything every day like we did. I was surprised because I had always believed you had to knock yourself out to improve.' Pagey, driven by his perceived inadequacy in certain of the events, continued to train as hard as ever but Peter gradually learned to tone things down. It didn't seem to affect his performance because the results are there for all to see. You don't go to five Olympics without putting in the effort at training. As for the technique of tapering before a big event, Dunc didn't adopt that routine until he took up powerlifting thirty years later – in his fifties!

When asked to evaluate his time in Texas, Dunc flatly states, 'I couldn't have done it without Fort Sam. We were still feeling our way, but they showed us all the basics of what to do – all the little things that helped.' This was particularly the case in the ride and the shoot where the hard days and hot nights seemed to have brought immediate benefits. Pagey listened carefully to Colonel Russell's wise counsel on how to approach the ride and it paid off immediately. George Murley's coaching resulted in major changes in the shoot. Pete and Dunc, acting on his advice, changed over to using the Smith and Wesson K22 pistols supplied by the US Army instead of the firearms they brought with them. It was a much more reliable pistol and made one less of the 'terrible lot' of things that could go wrong when lining up a target. Pagey says that George was much more than just 'a good old boy' who every now and then brought watermelons to training, because when he got down to business his coaching and advice was an immeasurable help to his newfound Aussie mates.

Pete and Dunc hadn't been training long before things got really serious. Fort Sam played host to an annual event known as the May Comp. The army invited South American countries to compete in a Modern Pentathlon event – 'It was the only comp they all came up for . . . Mexico, Argentina and Brazil . . . you name it, they all showed up.' Pagey is unclear about the exact date, but it fits nicely with the Mexican and south Texas celebration of Cinco de Mayo which nowadays is a major event. The Fifth of May commemorates the date in 1862 when the Mexican Army had a glorious victory over the French Army at the Battle of Puebla. Today the Cinco de Mayo celebration is so large that beer consumption is greater than either the Superbowl or St Patrick's Day. Back in the day there was no way the beer was flowing– at Fort Sam the May Comp was all business.

It was a five-day event held every year – for North and South American countries it was the real deal for Modern Pentathlon. As always things started off with the ride and, on that day, things went exceptionally well for Dunc. The course was challenging and it required the riders to guide their horses through scrub and bush and trees. Pagey describes the terrain as not too dissimilar to the Australian bush. 'We walked the course beforehand, so we knew what was coming, but you could see some of the others were pretty worried.' And worried they should have been – as well as having to negotiate The Slide, they also had to take their mounts over a jump known as 'The Piano Bench' before swimming them across Salado Creek to the finish. The very idea of a piano bench on a pentathlon cross country equestrian course seems incongruous but there is a twisted logic to it. Try to imagine a very large grand piano. Ride across that, and then descend to the equally large keys. After landing safely there, go straight to the bench and then jump down to the floor. The Piano Bench was a descending series of jumps that challenged both horse and rider. 'In all the courses we rode around the world we never came across another jump like "The Piano Bench" at Fort Sam.'

When the time came for the anxious riders to enter the lottery of picking their mounts, Dunc put his hand in the hat and drew a number. He remembers his horse's name to this day – 'It was called Pharaoh'. As he was saddling up, Colonel Russel walked past and asked, 'Do you know what you've got there Dunc?' Pagey had no idea but he wasn't about to show his ignorance to his mentor. It turned out that Pharaoh was a pretty good horse. 'We went around the course with no problems.' Other riders didn't share in their good fortune. Peter had a particularly difficult ride. Things got really interesting when his mount's front feet got stuck in the mud after they jumped into Salado Creek. Pete wound up doing an impressive somersault over the horse's head and landed safely in the creek. When he hit the water, he instinctively dived for the bottom and hung onto some reeds while his horse flailed about in the water above. Dunc laughs as he recalls that when Peter's mount finished sorting itself out, the submerged rider popped up to the surface like a deep-sea diver. Once all riders had completed the course, and allowance was made for the unfortunates who hadn't, the blow-in from Australia was declared the winner. Duncan Page had won the ride at the May Comp. Before he mounted the podium to accept the accolades, an Aussie soldier on an official visit to Fort Sam walked up and said, 'Here, wear this'. He handed Dunc his slouch hat complete with puggaree and badge. Duncan stood tall and proudly wore one of his country's most cherished symbols as he received the applause.

The generous Digger reclaimed his hat before Pagey was given a far less genteel form of recognition. A longstanding tradition for the winner of the ride is that he is thrown into Salado Creek. That year it was the Mexican team's honour to take Dunc by his arms and legs and, with great ceremony, toss him in the muddy water. It may have been the Cinco de Mayo spirit, or most likely the Mexicans getting their own back on a gringo, but Dunc found himself summarily plunged into the depths of the watercourse he and the others had recently ridden across. A thoroughly dishevelled and mud splattered winner scrambled up the banks and out of the creek. He sat down on a nearby log and asked Peter to help him out of his squelching riding boots. Pete cheerfully obliged and returned to the creek to wash the muck and mud off his hands. Once there, he didn't tarry long because when he dipped his hands in the water, he saw to his horror that the creek was alive with wriggling water moccasins, or cotton mouths – a particularly lethal snake common to that part of the world. It was the same place where Pagey had just clambered out. As for Pete, who witnessed first-hand the reptilian takeover of Salado Creek, his hands went unwashed until he returned to quarters.

Asked about his performance on the following days, Duncan rated himself as 'very average'. With the benefit of retrospect, he now accepts that the training at Fort Sam was of immense benefit to his performance in all areas – 'Everything you did improved you as an experience'. All in all, the best year of Pagey's life was a more than adequate preparation for what was lay before him.

15

THE PEOPLE YOU MEET

Modern Pentathlon was a magnet for the kind of man possessed of a unique personality – and it was almost always a strong personality. While Fort Sam was first and foremost a military base, not all the pentathletes in its bachelor quarters were cut from the same cloth as General George Patton. Enlisted man or draftee, how they got there didn't substantially affect their view of life or the behaviour that flowed from it. Hear it from Duncan himself: 'Most of the fellows were real individuals, and to do that sport you had to be an individual. Everyone in his own way was a character.' Several decades after his years there, Duncan harbours fond memories of the men he encountered at Fort Sam. Strong personalities seemed to spring from the fort's very soil and their attitude was contagious. The Texas of the time was never backward in bragging about itself – everything in The Lone Star State was bigger and better than anywhere else. When the much larger Alaska was given statehood in 1959, Texans grudgingly conceded that, while it may be bigger, the Lone Star state was still the best.

Very few of the pentathletes at Fort Sam were native Texans. In fact, as you would expect in the military, the men were drawn from all points of the compass and from all walks of life. The common denominator linking them was Modern Pentathlon and an ironclad determination to excel in the discipline which gave them joint purpose. Given that Pete and Dunc's training companions were from widely divergent backgrounds it followed that many of them were unique individuals – some extremely unique – who manifested a wide range of behavioural idiosyncrasies. Pagey recalls many of his training mates with genuine nostalgia. His reminiscences often start off with 'and then there was . . .' or 'how could you forget . . .' A few of the 'how could you forgets' come up again and again. In a moment of reflection, he once said, 'When you look at it, all those pentathlon guys were larger than life. And in some ways, all of them were very odd people.' The exceptions being Peter and himself, he is quick to add.

No matter what you say about Texas or Texans and their penchant for telling tall tales, there is no denying that they are a hospitable people – often to a fault. The generous Army Sergeant Gil Gunderson and his wife are a prime example. Upon hearing that there were a couple of Aussies living on the base, the couple introduced themselves and set about showing Pete and Dunc some good ole Texas hospitality. They boys struggled to find a way to reciprocate the Gunderson's kindness, until a golden opportunity arrived out of the blue. Fort Sam has its own golf course. Of course it did – it is the US Army. Gil Gunderson, like many of his compatriots, was an avid golfer. That year the course played host to a PGA tournament and it so happened that Bruce Crampton, who was on a career high, headlined the field. Pagey still has no idea how he managed it, but somehow he caught up with his Beverley Park mate and they arranged to meet for dinner the night before the tournament. Peter and Duncan invited Gil and his wife along and, fortunately for the impoverished pair, a star-struck sergeant insisted on paying the bill.

Pagey remembers the restaurant vividly. It was one of those places where the chief item on the menu was a massive piece of meat described as a 'steak' which came with all the trimmings. The challenge was – leave a clean plate and patron could eat for nothing. 'The steak was huge. There was no way I could get through all that, so I didn't try', says Duncan. The dinner went well. The Australian professional golfer, normally a reserved person, was at his affable best; while Gil Gunderson, amateur golfer but major fan, was in hog heaven. For Gil, the best was yet to come. The next morning while standing on the first tee before he was to hit off, Bruce surveyed the crowd and spotted his host from the night before. He made a point of walking over to say 'g'day' and thank Gil for his generous hospitality. Pagey is sure 'Bruce did that deliberately' and it was a fine gesture because it transported Gil to fairway heaven. His mates crowded around demanding to know how he came to know Bruce Crampton. It was a major feather in his golf cap because as

Pagey says, 'After all, Bruce was a big deal in those days'. So there you are – the time Dunc spent at Beverley Park paid off in spades for one lucky American soldier who now had one up on his golfing buddies. It also helped two very thankful Aussies to reciprocate a kindness.

It was probably foreordained long before he got to Texas that Duncan Page would run into Colonel Charles Askins of the US Army and Border Patrol distinction. Both men shared an interest in the artistry as well as the mechanics of pistol shooting. The good Colonel won many championships over many years during the time he served his state and his country. Duncan had dreams of doing something similar for his own country although in more pacific circumstances. Colonel Askins was the father of Bill, one of Dunc's fellow pentathletes and they became firm friends during the time they trained at Fort Sam. Young Bill often took Pagey home to meet his famous father. The Colonel couldn't help but notice his young guest's interest in firearms, and occasionally shared some episodes from his legendary career. Although he served under George Patton as an ordnance officer in WWII, his most lurid tales came from his days in the US Border Patrol hunting down rumrunners trying to slip into Texas along the Rio Grande.

It doesn't take much imagination to picture a wide-eyed Pagey listening to the colonel's tall but true tales. Those he remembers most vividly are the man's recollections of his time in the Border Patrol when he stalked and apprehended smugglers along the famous waterway that defines the border between Texas and Mexico. Colonel Askins was a prolific writer on the subject of firearms. He called his autobiography *Unrepentant Sinner* and, from what is contained its pages, the title is not too far from the truth. Dunc recalls the colonel telling him that, all up, he must have been involved in over fifty gunfights. One visit to the Colonel's home office revealed a glass-fronted cabinet with handguns of all descriptions on display. When asked why he kept them, Charles Askins looked up from his desk and in an off-handed tone said, 'Oh those are the firearms I took from the men I shot'.

As for the colonel's son, Bill Askins, it didn't take long before Dunc realised that the apple hadn't fallen far from the tree. Askins Junior had a burning ambition to see service in Viet Nam, which at the time, was starting to heat up. 'All he wanted to do was go to Viet Nam and fly a helicopter gunship.' As for Bill's present ambitions, the aspiring chopper pilot had to settle for a Porsche which he drove with considerable abandon around San Antonio and surrounding areas. Dunc recalls one night cruising with his mate through the centre of San Antone when Bill spotted a jackrabbit minding its own business in one of the city's many parks. He reached into the car door compartment and pulled out a pistol. He then proceeded to let fly in the general direction of the rabbit. After he emptied the magazine and while the shots still echoing, Bill looked at Dunc and said in his dry Texas drawl, 'We'd better get the hell out of here'. He floored the Porsche and took off while his astonished passenger tried to come to grips with what he had seen. 'I couldn't believe it. It was like shooting at something in the middle of Sydney.'

If Askins and son weren't sufficiently rugged as individuals, Dunc reminisces about a character of an altogether different stripe, the long and lanky Bob Beck. Colonel Russell, with Stetson on head and cigar in hand, declared that, as far as he could tell, Bob Beck would either wind up 'president of the United States or behind bars for life'. Before he came to pentathlon, Bob had completed a degree in dentistry and, unlike many of the others, he had a career waiting. Dunc didn't find Bob Beck a particularly friendly fellow on first impressions. He could see that relations between Bob and the other pentathletes were at times 'quite frosty'. The dentist cum pentathlete was 'used to doing what he wanted to do and there was always a certain aloofness to him', according to Pagey. This was particularly the case with the other American pentathletes where competition for a place on the team could be quite willing. As for the Aussies, once Bob understood that they were not an immediate threat, things became reasonably amicable. So much so that, on those endlessly hot Texas nights, he would come by the boys' rooms and ask, 'Do you guys want to go out for a ride?' Then he, his wife, Roma, Pete and Dunc would sneak down to the stables, saddle up a horse and trot out for a midnight ride. 'It was strictly against regulations of course, but that was Bob.' They would ride down Broadway in San Antone, cross the deserted highway and head over to the Polo Grounds. Anything to beat the heat.

Dunc recalls that Bob was a good fencer and one of the few to adopt his French coach's preferred grip. Beck's long arms made him a formidable opponent. He was a cautious and defensive fencer and a powerful swimmer, one of only two in that era who had broken the four-minute barrier in the pentathlon swim at the Rome Olympics. Despite his undoubted ability, 'Bob was always trying to play the angles'. He was a better than average rider, but he wanted to lock in his edge on rest of the competition. The day before the ride, and after the riders had completed their preliminary walk of the course, it wasn't unknown for the Becks – husband and wife – to return to measure the distance between jumps. They would then drag away any obstructing brush to give Bob a shorter run-up once the whips got cracking. As for fencing, there Beck's skulduggery was more sophisticated. He reverted to his skills as a qualified dentist and applied his dental tools to customise his épée. The end result was that he believed that his alterations gave an advantage over the other competitors. An explanation of what he did it is far too long and convoluted to bother with here. Nor is it of interest to anyone but a Musketeer. It is enough that Bob believed they gave him a jump on the others and that was all that really mattered.

'All in all, we got on quite well with Bob Beck.' Pete and Dunc's long and lean mate was always forthcoming with insider advice to give them a leg up when they competed against his American rivals. Anything to help Bob's chances of making the team. Colonel Russell's assessment of his lanky student's future wasn't too far from the mark. A quick glance at the *San Antonio Express-News* of February 10, 2015, shows the aging but still long and upright Bob Beck leaving Federal Court. It seems he was in dispute with the Internal Revenue Service about the small matter of an alleged tax debt to the tune of 4.3 million dollars. It is tempting to picture the Colonel emitting a deep sigh as he puts down the paper, takes the cigar from his mouth and nods knowingly at the horse statues arrayed across his mantlepiece.

We now move on to a gentleman from the Naval Academy at Annapolis by way of Tucson, Arizona. In his university days, first at Yale and then Annapolis, Al Morales had been a fine lacrosse player and sabre fencer. Somewhere along the way he decided to take up Modern Pentathlon. Al arrived at Fort Sam shortly after Pete and Dunc. Pagey remembers him as a 'flinty customer' but said that they got along quite well. Al had a significant advantage over the others – as the reigning national inter-collegiate sabre champion, he knew he was going to the Olympics no matter how he fared at Fort Sam.

His first day at the base started off as all days did – with the ride. The colonel assumed his normal position on top of a large rock, adjusted his Stetson and addressed his protégés. 'Okay boys, go out there and find a horse you think you can ride.' The colonel then looked at the newcomer and said, 'Al, if you wouldn't mind, I'd like a word with you'. Al complied of course – no one said 'no' to Colonel Russell. The 'word' stretched into several and, by the time Al arrived to pick his mount, there was only one horse left – 'Big Jim'. Unlike many of the others, Dunc selected a different horse every day in an effort to accustom himself to the vagaries of the equine species. He knew Big Jim and knew what to expect – somewhere along the course the bloody thing would either stumble unexpectedly or collapse in a heap. 'No one wanted to ride him because he would always stumble and fall. Al Morales, innocent newbie that he was, had no idea what he was getting into as he mounted up and caught up with the others.

Big Jim behaved exactly as predicted. Al steered the horse over the first jump which was a drop jump. And a drop jump is? Good question – a jump that starts on level ground and, as the name suggests, drops to a level below where you started. In Dunc's words, 'It's a jump where you take off higher than where you land'. With Al temporarily mounted on his back, Big Jim took off with a mighty leap and then, finding no ground beneath him, performed up to expectations – he promptly collapsed and fell in a heap. Big Jim's rider, totally unprepared for his mount's response, was catapulted into thin air. 'Al went flying and all the guys had a good laugh.' After they finished the ride, they loaded the horses on what Dunc describes as a 'massive float'. Unfortunately, there was not enough room left for Big Jim and Pagey's horse, so the colonel asked Dunc and Al to ride back to the stables by way of the golf course. Somewhere on the way the boys challenged each other to a race to the top of a hill. The Aussie got a good jump on the Yank and charged up to the slope finishing a clear winner. At the peak of the hill, Dunc turned to look for Al but all he saw was a riderless Big Jim clumping up to join him. A slightly concerned Pagey retraced their tracks but, after a long look around, found no sign of Al, so he headed the horses back to the stables. Along the way he was overtaken by a fast-moving Army jeep. The passenger in the back who waved merrily at Dunc was none other than Al Morales, presumably grateful to be without the encumbrance of the erratic Big Jim.

'Al was always a confident guy. He knew he was going to make the sabre fencing team. It gave him the confidence that, whatever happened in pentathlon, he was going to the Olympics no matter what.' By the end of his sporting career, Al Morales had in fact gone to the Olympics – he represented his country a grand total of four times. Not a bad effort for a guy who took up pentathlon almost as an afterthought. 'We finished up being quite good mates but there was always a slight edge to him.'

Good enough mates that Al had no hesitation introducing Peter to an attractive lady friend of his and left things to develop from there. The lady in question was quite a looker and Pete thought he might like to get to know her better. She had no objections and, better still, she came with her own transport – Pete didn't need the Cadillac. On their first date things went well enough so they agreed that a second was a good idea. The early buzz came with a rosy glow until Peter asked if she had any tissues. 'They're in the glove compartment', was the direction. Tissues located; the passenger couldn't help but notice a silver pistol resting elegantly beside them. Immediately on the alert, Pete asked, 'What's the pistol for?' It seemed a logical question under the circumstances. He didn't often encounter women with weapons. The answer, accompanied with a significant look, was blunt and to the point, 'There are a lot of bad hombres in this part of the world'. Peter recalls that as being the precise moment he decided that two dates with Al Morales' friend would probably do him.

A man with a different sort of edge who arrived at Fort Sam shortly after Peter and Duncan was Mike D'Asaro, the boy from Brooklyn, New York. The army sent Mike to Fort Sam with the expectation that he would develop into a pentathlete. He was a fencing opponent of Al Morales and the two of them ran neck and neck in the US sabre championships. Both men were excellent fencers, but the similarities stopped there. Where Al Morales had volunteered to serve his country, Mike was drafted. Where Al had a certain aloofness to him, Mike was affability itself. Dunc is adamant that Mike D'Asaro was 'the best sabre man to come out of America'. 'Like Nureyev' is his description of Mike's movements. Better still, the Brooklyn boy's ability was never accompanied by a big head or an inflated self-opinion. 'As good as he was in the épée, he never tried to show you up.' Dunc shows unfeigned enjoyment when he recalls Mike as 'a gregarious sort of soul' in that 'unique Italian-American way'. As an athlete, Mike could 'move across the ground amazingly'. He was reputedly a first-rate handball player – a minor sport that, as the years go by, is gaining in popularity and prominence. If fencing and handball were Mike's undeniable strengths, his pursuit of the other pentathlon skills were accompanied by some outstanding weaknesses.

In the fifties, the process of coming of age in Brooklyn didn't involve giving its younger citizens access to horse riding academies and swimming pools. And, as he was a typical kid in his neighbourhood, Mike's riding and swimming abilities were virtually non-existent when he showed up at Fort Sam. Not a huge recommendation for your average pentathlon aspirant. When asked about his ability in the pool, Dunc lets out a great whoop – 'Hopeless! But I guess there weren't a lot of swimming pools where he grew up'. As for his riding ability, he gives a quiet belly laugh and observes that 'Mike wasn't too keen on the horses, but then there weren't too many of them in Brooklyn either I suppose'. In the modest and non-judgemental manner that typifies him, Dunc notes that both skills are things you 'grow up with and he just didn't have the opportunities'.

But Mike persisted. He was no quitter, although the ride must have been a particularly difficult ordeal. Mike's son remembers his dad saying that he 'hated his equestrian coach'. It isn't too much of a stretch to imagine that the crusty Colonel Russell would have had little time for a genuinely inept pupil. In the end, the army suggested that Mike spend most of his time coaching and training his fellow fencers – indeed, that may have been the intention all along. No matter what his inadequacies, Mike D'Asaro is one of the Fort Sam people that Duncan remembers with great fondness and respect, both for his silky fencing skills and his determination to succeed in the pool and on the equestrian course.

Another pentathlete Dunc speaks of with immense respect is Lt Baisal D Smith, an army helicopter pilot. Baisal Smith was a strong Christian and a confirmed pacifist who refused to take part in regular combat duties, although he readily volunteered his skills to ferry wounded soldiers away from combat zones. There is a sketchy reference to Baisal as a pentathlete in an article in the local paper that has him running second in a pentathlon event for US athletes. Almost unbelievably, he ran second in that event to none other than Mike D'Asaro. The article notes that Al Morales, the heavy favourite, was disqualified in the run because he missed a gate. When informed of Al's mishap, Pagey, speaking from the voice of experience, laughed and said, 'It can happen mate. Anything that can go wrong, will go wrong.' Dunc's prime memory of Baisal Smith is of a man who was exceptionally courageous in his duty. He wouldn't fight but he never shied away from flying into the thick of things. 'He was a combat rescue pilot who wouldn't say "no" to any mission, and that takes some guts mate.'

Dunc recalls Baisal describing one particular mission where he had to fly into the middle of a firefight to retrieve a wounded soldier. In the process of the rescue, Baisal's helicopter was shot to ribbons and was unable to fly. The pilot had no option but to carry the patient on his back and he dragged him to the safety of the scrub that bordered the paddy where he had left the chopper. As he carried the wounded man out of the heat of battle, he heard him ask, 'What are you doing?' Baisal's hurried reply, conducted under incoming fire, went something like, 'I'm carrying you out of here buddy. We've got to get away fast'. The wounded soldier reacted with alacrity and said, 'The hell you are, I'm getting out of here myself'. He then proceeded to shake himself out of Baisal's grip and found that his wounds were miraculously healed as he sprinted for cover, leaving a world class pentathlete in his wake. As a sign of the bond that developed between Pagey and his American mate, Baisal and his wife, while on holiday in Sydney during the late sixties, made a special effort to Blakehurst. At last Dunc could return some of the hospitality that had been lavished on Peter and himself during their time at Fort Sam.

Pagey remembers with great humour an episode involving another of his pentathlete mates, Davis Moberly. At the time Davis was a lowly private in the US army. The rank is important to what is to unfold. The private was a 'fair to middlin' pentathlete who couldn't swim but 'rode well'. So well in fact that he came second to Dunc in his win at the May Comp. Upon occasion, Davis, like all riders, would have a bad day or experience bad luck at the jumps around the course. One particular day turned out to be a shocker for Private Moberly when he came off his mount at a particularly difficult jump. He sailed through the air, landed awkwardly and broke his collarbone. The bone was set the next day at Fort Sam by a captain in the medical service. Davis left the hospital with strict instructions to remain inactive and report back in three weeks. The plaster cast stretched from neck to mid-waist and soon became a constant irritant to the active young man. Private Moberly duly reported back to the Captain Doctor and informed him that he felt his injury had healed and requested to be allowed to resume pentathlon training. The stinging response from the medical officer went something like, 'I will be the one to tell you when you've healed, private'. Military pecking order thus restored, the doc ordered the suitably chastened private to report back in two weeks.

The medic should have known better. Davis Moberly, like most young men in the prime of life, never intended to remain immobile for a minute longer than he had to. It didn't matter what the doctor said, young Davis was adamant that he would be the one to decide when he had healed. Pete and Dunc, who had befriended him early on, were his willing accomplices. Somehow they managed to lay hands on a pair of bolt cutters and performed surgery on the back of the cast. They then carefully removed it from the patient and stood it in the corner of his room. Pagey recalls the cast as looking 'exactly like Ned Kelly's armour'. The two week interim before the next appointment saw Davis resume normal activities, particularly swimming and sunning himself by the pool. On the day he was required to report back to the captain, Pete and Dunc replaced Ned Kelly's armour and carefully resealed it with plaster of Paris. They stood back for a quick look and noticed that the replaced plaster was too obvious. The Aussie accomplices hastily spread dirt over the new bits so they matched the rest of the, by then, thoroughly disreputable cast.

Again, Private Moberly presented himself and repeated his self-diagnosis: 'excellent'. The irritated medico was even more perfunctory this time around: 'I'll be the one to decide when you are healed Private'. The Aussie boys wasted no time restoring their mate to full mobility and he immediately resumed full pentathlon training. Ten days later a sun-tanned, fully recovered and fully fit private returned to the medic although not before Ned Kelly's armour was replaced – yet again. Today Pagey laughingly says, 'I have no idea what the doctor would have thought. Davis was as brown as a berry from top to bottom.' That episode is reflective of the joys of life at Fort Sam. The good times far outweighed the bad, and their lifelong friendships are testament to that.

There was a darker side to life in the United States as Pete and Dunc were to discover after they befriended David Kirkwood. Dave was an Olympic silver medallist in Modern Pentathlon, an officer in the United States Air Force and an African American. 'He was the first black American I'd ever met.' Pagey remembers Dave Kirkwood well and describes him as very precise in everything he did. 'He thought things through and was one of the few to use the grip recommended by the fencing coach. They got along extremely well – so much so that Peter and Duncan began to notice Dave's absence on certain occasions when they and the others socialised.

The local hangout for the Fort Sam pentathletes was called 'The Pig Stand' – a typical American burger joint they frequented in their spare time. Dave used to drive Pete and Dunc to The Pig Stand but declined their offer to come in and join them. After refusing a few times, the Aussies put it down to the fact that Dave just wasn't all that hungry. They soon found otherwise when one of the other Americans advised them not to invite Dave anymore because he wouldn't be served. 'We'd never experienced that before and decided then and there to quit going there.'

The Aussies' experience with discrimination didn't end at The Pig Stand; it continued insidiously at the Lone Star Brewery swimming pool. The Lone Star's saloon was decorated after the fashion of a classic old-style western saloon: swinging doors, a long bar and sepia pictures of San Antone during its Wild West days. Better still was the offer of free root beer for the pentathletes who flocked there after training. Again after a few forays into the saloon, the Aussies asked, 'Where's Dave?' Same response: 'Not allowed in here'. As with the previous venue, they immediately 'quit going there' and found a small room behind the brewery where Dave was allowed to join the others – which he did.

They eventually came upon a place that allowed Dave through the door – the front door at that. The new hangout where the pentathlon crew congregated on Saturday nights was called 'Mammy's'. It was a Mexican restaurant that had seen better days. A prime attraction was its waitstaff – numerous flashing eyed señoritas took orders and tolerated the customers' banter. The other attraction was the food. Not that Dunc remembers it as anything special, but Mammy's offered hungry young men an irresistible offer – all you can eat for one dollar. It was too good to refuse. For a measly buck the boys were up for the challenge and gave it their best shot. One man stood head and shoulders above the rest. Paul Pesthy was the son of a Hungarian fencer who won an

Olympic gold medal for his country. Paul was himself a fine fencer and he went on to win numerous American titles. As a pentathlete he represented his country with distinction. In a torrid competition with the others, Paul set a Mammy's record for polishing off forty plates of food in one sitting.

Paul Pesthy would go on to win medals in fencing and pentathlon but his degustation performance at Mammy's is generally considered his premier podium appearance. With all the hijinks and skylarking no one talked about race issues until an unusual conversation between Dunc and Dave Kirkwood. Pagey often mentions the energy-sapping heat during the training sessions at Fort Sam. After one such debilitating workout, Dunc threw himself down on a bench beside Dave and noticed his mate was sipping from a bottle of Coke. Without hesitation, he asked Dave if he could have a couple of swigs and was totally unprepared for his mate's response. At first it was a look of 'absolute shock' and then Dave handed over the bottle in 'a bemused sort of way'. Dunc took a couple of grateful swigs and handed the Coke bottle back. Dave then informed him that it was 'the first time a white guy has ever drunk out of the same bottle as me'. 'I didn't really understand it at the time. After all we swam in the same pool and ate at the same table.' Dunc also mentioned that a few of the pentathletes wouldn't even talk to Dave. 'That was their way mate.' It may have been their way, but it certainly wasn't the way for Duncan and Peter who, then as they do today, consider a mate to be a mate irrespective of his skin colour.

Many more tales of life at Fort Sam remain but it is best to leave them at the Mexican border. And that is exactly where the ever-generous Dave Kirkwood dropped the Aussies off. Pete and Dunc gratefully thanked their American mate and boarded the train that would take them to the 1962 Modern Pentathlon World Championships in Mexico City.

16

SOUTH OF THE BORDER

It was hell for leather. Don McMiken was on a mission as he pushed his horse around the course at a breakneck pace. This was Don's big chance. He was competing in the Australian Modern Pentathlon Championships and a lot was riding (literally) on his performance. It meant either going to the World Championships in Mexico with the boys from Fort Sam or staying home and training on. That day Don won the ride by minutes over the other competitors, including Terry Nicholl – the competitor jocularly referred to as 'Freddy the Fibber' because of his extravagant tales about his alleged exploits. It was at this precise moment the personage of John Xavier O'Driscoll comes into the picture. O'Driscoll, a prominent figure in the Melbourne legal world, was non-competing captain of the pentathlon team at Rome and later stayed on as a decision-making administrator. On that occasion, the august O'Driscoll was among the officials responsible for tallying the results.

To this day, Duncan shakes his head as he retells the story of the haphazard decision that denied his mate his first opportunity to represent his country. Don won the ride with a minute and a half to spare over the nearest competitor. No one else was even close. His family, themselves well-versed in matters equestrian, also timed his ride. But as was to happen time after time for the Australian pentathletes, and Don in particular, the 'powers that be', proudly attired in official blazers, right royally stuffed things up. The decision makers, John Xavier O'Driscoll included, determined that Don's time for the ride must have been incorrect. Somehow the timer must have made a mistake. There is no way McMiken (they always used surnames) could have been that much quicker than the others. These late afternoon deliberations, possibly aided by a hip flask containing some form of spirituous beverage, concluded that the only thing to do was to add a minute to Don's ride. The revised time meant that the winning rider was denied a place on the team. Consequently, he would be going to the world championships, but only as a reserve. Don was left off the team in favour of the loquacious Terry Nicholl. The blazers had decreed that all decisions were final, and no further discussion would be entered into. This was despite the McMiken family's evidence that the original time was correct. Pagey smiles sourly when he comments about the incident – 'It was Rafferty's rules back then mate. In fact, it was Hicksville.' The results were in – the boys in blazers, one; McMiken, zero.

The name John Xavier O'Driscoll pops up again and again in the pentathlon tales. Dunc describes him as a 'tall, large man with a belly. He had a bulbous red nose and was a bit of a drinker.' The judge was president of the Australian Modern Pentathlon Association and didn't mind who knew it. 'He was the type of bloke who wanted people to know who was running the show and always wanted to be right.' Dunc remembers O'Driscoll as being stern and authoritarian toward all the pentathletes, and to Don in particular. Don McMiken has never been the kind of man to back down, especially to someone capable of making capricious and arbitrary decisions that directly affected his future. In consequence, the two men reached a standoff – 'Don didn't like him, and the Judge didn't like Don.' As the years went on, the mutual animosity continued. Don was never backward in telling Xavier O'Driscoll exactly what he thought of him. There is one incident that is typical of the many decisions inflicted on the pentathletes. There is one identifying feature that is increasingly apparent when Pagey starts reminiscing. The administrators of Australian sport, instead of facilitating the progress of athletes, seemed to take delight in making things difficult. It's a wonder that men like Page, Macken and McMiken persisted. It is to their credit that they did. Their ironclad commitment never wavered.

Pagey saw O'Driscoll's authoritarian streak firsthand the day he and John Winchester caught up with each other at a pentathlon competition. John was an international equestrian athlete, a three day event rider who represented Australia at the Melbourne Games in Stockholm, Sweden. Wait a minute – the Melbourne Olympics in Sweden? That's correct – in Sweden. Australia's stringent quarantine laws required Melbourne's equestrian events to be held offshore and Stockholm was the pick. In the fifties the very thought of foreign livestock bringing exotic diseases into the country had quarantine agents wringing their hands. So John Winchester and the rest of the equestrian team did their bit for Australia in Sweden.

Now back to O'Driscoll, who was occupying a prominent position atop an old bullock dray at the edge of the riding course. Loud hailer in hand, the large man with the red nose barked out orders in a magisterial voice. Pagey and John were well within hearing distance as he issued his lordly instructions: 'Rider, you will approach the next jump and fifty yards after that you will turn right.' Several other directions were added until, unable to contain himself, John Winchester shouted out, 'He can't do that'. The judge ignored the objection and carried on, oblivious to interjections from an equestrian athlete who actually knew the rules.

Still in Mexico and oblivious to the travails of their mate at home, the boys were on a train to Mexico City, staring steadily out the window at the arid scenery. Dunc remembers it was 'just like you see it in the movies. At every stop you would see men sitting under their sombreros having a siesta in the shade.' Pagey, who was familiar with the exploits of the Mexican nationalist Pancho Villa, half expected to see the notorious general, rifle in hand, leading his band of revolutionaries in a headlong gallop alongside the train. The villainous Pancho failed to show and the train ground its way unhindered by bandidos into the heights of Mexico City where two travel weary Aussies gratefully disembarked.

Ah, Mexico. Or as the locals say the word, 'Meh-hee-co'. Who would have thought Duncan Page would find himself strolling the byways of Mexico City? But there he was, strongly resisting the impulse to pinch himself. A couple of years ago the best he could do was mope around the house and limp from one room to another. Now, thanks to Fort Sam and its rigorous training regime, he was wearing the green and gold – a proud and deserving member of the Australian Modern Pentathlon team. Pagey had finally cracked it – here he was at the World Pentathlon Championships.

Although he would strenuously object, Duncan Page is a sentimentalist at heart – just put 'I Can't Stop Loving You' on the stereo and watch him melt. Dunc is also a big fan of Willie Nelson and he particularly enjoys Ole Willie's version of 'South of the Border'. Pagey's trips to Mexico – one for the World Championships and a second for the 1968 Olympics obviously contributed to his affection for the country. It may also have something to do with the lovely señorita Maria Elena, whose memory can also turn him misty eyed. Maria Elena? The señorita's surname is of no consequence, and Pagey can't remember how to spell it anyway. The story goes that while he and Pete were sightseeing in Mexico City, they chanced upon a group of señoritas amusing themselves in a lovely, shady park. As young people do, they struck up a conversation. Luckily, Maria Elena spoke fluent English – her grandfather was English. One thing led to another, and Señor Page asked the enchanting señorita if she would like to go out with him. The invitation was shyly accepted. The handsome gringo was asked to pick her up at 6:30 pm that night.

Showered, shaved and immaculately presented, the eager suitor knocked on the front door of the grand hacienda at the arranged time. He was met by a demure Maria Elena and a forbidding older sister. The conversation was polite, if somewhat stilted, and finally ended when Dunc politely asked the older sister what time she expected Maria Elena home. The sister consulted her watch and said, 'I would like my sister home by 7:30 pm'. That left little time to get to know each other, so they raced off to the Latin American building. At the time it was the tallest building in the city. They went straight to the top, had one soft drink, and raced back home before the curfew bell tolled.

As you would expect, the formidable older sister was watching and waiting when Dunc returned Maria Elena safely home. And this is where the story takes a twist. The sister asked the gringo gentleman if he would escort her to the shops as she needed to purchase a loaf of bread. Pagey gallantly complied. The loaf was obtained, and the sister pulled the car up outside the front gate.

SOUTH OF THE BORDER

The gate was large and solidly constructed. Cast iron in fact. Dunc knew what was expected. He got out and, with some difficulty, swung it open. She drove through and turned to watch Dunc shut the gate. It was heavy and difficult to close, so the best option was to go outside and pull it shut. No sooner had he done so, the sister swung the large iron bolt across the gate leaving Pagey well and truly on the outer.

Despite the emphatic thump that ended the first date, the relationship somehow continued for the duration of the championships. Maria Elena graciously showed her squire the highlights of Mexico City. They went to the bullfights, the floating gardens and did all the touristy things that people do. As always, there was the matter of money. For as long as he was involved with Modern Pentathlon, Duncan Page was perpetually broke. The Pentathlon association was notoriously, and upon occasion, maliciously tight-fisted. Pagey was doing Mexico on a shoestring. And this is where his companion's local knowledge was of inestimable value. He and Maria Elena went to the bullfights and Dunc asked, 'How much?' The ticket guy said, 'Five pesos, señor'; with flashing eyes Maria Elena replied, 'Give him two'. It went like that every time Pagey dipped into his wallet and he laughs when he recalls that happy time. 'She saved me heaps and I needed it.' When it came time for the boys to leave town after the championships, the señorita's pennywise approach ensured that a few pesos remained in his back pocket.

Romance was nice, but it wasn't at the top of his to-do list. There remained the small matter of the world championships to consider. Pagey did well in the ride, finishing fourth overall, but the team as a whole performed poorly. Their results weren't helped by the generally unhelpful attitude of the team's discontented reserve. The idea was that the fourth member would assist the others in all manner of ways. That wasn't the way Don McMiken saw it. 'He was still smarting that Terry was in the team and not him.' The legitimately cranky Don was generally uncooperative. Still, Dunc is adamant that it had nothing to do with the team's mediocre performance. 'Remember, this is the early days. It was the team's first international competition together, so there was nothing spectacular in what we did.'

The ceremony held the day before the ride always made for a fine spectacle. The competitors gathered together and waited for things to start. It is traditional for the host nation to send a rider around the course before the actual competition and demonstrate how it can be navigated successfully. The rider who had the honour that day was an immaculately dressed Mexican army officer mounted on a magnificent black horse – 'a real charger'. Off went 'el capitan' and his splendid mount. He would show the world that Mexican horsemanship has no equal. Well, it didn't quite work out that way. The ride usually takes about seven and a half minutes and, four minutes into it, the Mexican officer was well out of sight. It was then the competitors heard the ambulance sirens coming closer until it sounded like they were coming from somewhere out on the course. 'We raced up to the top of a hill to see what was going on', Dunc remembers. There, below them at one of the particularly difficult jumps – the 'Road Double' – lay the prostrate army officer and his black horse. The horse didn't make it but the officer was resuscitated by the paramedics. Dunc stoically insists that the carnage didn't overly frighten him for his own safety, 'but it put the willies up a lot of the others'.

Among 'the others' was the South African contingent which, after walking around the course, returned to their accommodation shaken to the core. They then sat down to compose final letters to their parents and loved ones. They, and a few other competitors, were particularly concerned by an obstacle that involved vaulting a small jump behind which lay a gully, about a yard wide, with a drop of fifty or sixty feet. Dunc chuckles when he recalls the reaction of some of the more fainthearted competitors. It didn't worry most of us, 'only the people who weren't good riders'. Pagey may have slept soundly the night before, but there were many riders who didn't. The sight of the Mexican army officer being carted off in an ambulance left night-time nerves jangling in the thin Mexican air.

When questioned about his attitude to the inevitable mishaps with horses, Pagey is philosophical. 'Falls happen all the time. Anyone who rides horses knows that you're going to fall now and then. It can happen. It's part of the game, especially if you're taking a horse over the jumps. You can't help bad luck mate.' A healthy acceptance of the realities of cross-country riding coupled with the solid coaching of Colonel Russell, improved Dunc's performance immeasurably. His fourth-place ride in Mexico was one of the team's few highlights. Although for the team as a whole, it was the beginning of better things to come.

Dunc can now joke that a major blessing of the Mexican adventure was the team's ability to escape the dreaded 'turista', or Montezuma's revenge – the gastrointestinal disorder that brings down many visitors to Mexico. Pagey has no idea how they avoided the affliction, given his first-hand observations of Mexican food hygiene. On his way to Maria Elena's hacienda one sunny afternoon, he happened upon a woman preparing taco shells. She laid them out carefully on the footpath and draped them over the kerb so they would take on the correct shape. That was mind boggling enough for the meticulously sanitary Duncan Page, but what transpired next is burnt into his memory. After the taco lady returned to her shop, Dunc watched a neighbourhood dog approach and size up the neat row of drying taco shells. The dog stopped, sniffed cautiously and then did what dogs do when nature calls. One leg was lifted and the canine applied a liquid garnish to the sunbaking pastry items. While he makes no reference to what he had for dinner with Maria Elena, we can be one hundred per cent certain it wasn't tacos.

Soon it was time to leave Mexico and, for what was not to be the last time, the team was let down badly by the pentathlon association. For some reason, the blazer-wearers expected athletes to pay for their own accommodation. The manager of the hotel had been circling. He knew potential absconders when he saw them. And he was bang on the money – or the lack of it. The pentathlon supremos gave the boys virtually no financial support. Dunc candidly admits that he and his mates were little more than penniless indigents forced onto the athletic breadline. 'We were just bums mate. We were just bumming our way around the world.' Things were so dire that sometimes, simply in order to compete, the boys had to scavenge used equipment – 'We used cast off equipment from the Yanks and the Brits. There were times when we wouldn't have survived if it wasn't for food handouts from them.' Dunc may have been holding the Australian flag, but the boys in blazers allowed other countries to pay their way.

If necessity is the mother of invention, then it is equally true that poverty is the father of ingenuity. For the boys it was always a matter of needs must. And this time the need was acute. The Three Amigos had a problem. The hotel manager was on to them, so how to do a bolt from the hotel and catch a train out of the country? With bags, gear, souvenirs crammed into a couple of taxis, they did a runner. In the mad dash for the train station, somehow Peter misplaced his pistol. He thought he may have dropped it somewhere on the station platform, so he raced around looking for it. In a mild panic, the others followed suit. At last, just as the train was pulling out, Don loudly informed Pete that he had discovered the missing firearm. By now the train was picking up pace. Peter had to run flat chat and take a flying leap onto the last of the northbound carriages. Dunc says, 'It was just like you see in the movies, when the hero jumps on the back of the train. The last carriage had a cow catcher on it, and that was what Pete landed on.' Just like Butch Cassidy, Pete worked his way along the side of the carriage until he could climb in through a window.

The Pentathlon Three, Dunc, Pete and Don – were bound for the security of Fort Sam where they could at least get a feed. As for Pagey himself, each turn of the wheels on the ribbon of steel sent the flashing eyes of Maria Elena further into the distance. So much for their first foray into Mexico – and now the boys could let out a collective sigh of relief and say, 'Adios amigo' and 'Hasta la vista'.

17

STONEY MOTHERLESS

If stone motherless broke was the natural state of the Pentathlon Three, they could at least relax and catch their breath in the welcoming confines of Fort Sam. The boys got straight back into full training and Don, who was an unofficial guest, fitted in like a hand in a glove. That was all well and good until, out of the blue, he came down with hepatitis. At the time, Fort Sam was reputed to have the largest military hospital in the world. The quality of care was excellent, although hepatitis was not nearly as well-researched as it is today. The recommended treatment was for complete bed rest – lots of it, and in a darkened room. Pete and Dunc were regular visitors although, after a couple of weeks, Don became increasingly stroppy. The medicos insisted that their Aussie patient must adhere to instructions but Don had other ideas. He had no intention of following standard medical procedure. The place was driving him nuts. One way or another, he had to get out of there. Don knew that if he did a runner, there no way he could remain at Fort Sam as an escaped patient. He soon found a willing accomplice. Davis Moberly, himself no stranger to medical authoritarianism, crept into Don's room one night, found him some clothes and crept back out with the absconding patient in tow. For Davis, it was a matter of one good deed deserved another. The Aussies had looked after him in his hour of need and he was more than happy to return the favour. That was one part of it – the thrill of the chase was the other. For adventurous young men in the prime of their lives, no obstacle was too great to overcome.

With Don's escape the Australian diaspora began. After Davis Moberly sprang him out of medical detention, he hopped on a Greyhound which took him to New York City. From there he caught a ship to England where he was now a problem for the Poms. Peter remained at Fort Sam a while longer but soon he was hitchhiking across the States (a far safer proposition in the sixties than it is today). He got to New York and boarded a ship to England where he caught up with Don. Duncan made his way back to Australia via San Diego. He carried with him an overnight bag that held roughly twenty thousand rounds of ammunition 'borrowed' from Fort Sam. He set about acquiring it systematically and methodically. Every time he shot, Dunc sequestered away any unspent ammo for later use. He had several willing accomplices – 'Every now and then, Davis or one of the others would bring me a box of ammunition'. Soon enough he had racked up twenty thousand rounds in the process. 'A man's got to do what a man's got to do', grins Duncan.

The contraband ammo constituted a logistical problem. The overnight bag weighed a fair bit and he had to wrestle it onto the ship. A fellow passenger noticed Duncan's struggles and asked if 'he had robbed Fort Knox'. The curious passenger wasn't too far from the truth. For Dunc, the ammunition was indeed a form of gold. Ammo wasn't cheap and it was essential for the constant practice so vital to improved shooting. One thing was certain – that kind of help wasn't forthcoming from the pentathlon association. Yet again, it was a simple matter of needs must. But there still remained the small problem of getting all that ammunition into the country.

Duncan's financial woes were never more evident than during the voyage home from San Diego. Somehow, he scratched together the fare, and that accounted for his accommodation and meals. The accommodation was basic – just above steerage – and he shared a cabin with four strangers. Pagey is philosophical about it, 'That's just the way it was in those days. It didn't seem anything unusual.' In his slender wallet Dunc carried the princely sum of five American dollars which had to last him all the way to Sydney. Three weeks on five bucks? Good luck with that. Despite his best intentions, the five dollars vanished after a few days and he was confronted with grim reality – he was stony motherless broke. So broke that he was reduced to scrounging for half-used tubes of toothpaste and any soap that passengers left behind in the bathrooms. 'That was long before AIDS mate' – says the always stringently hygienic Mr Page.

What to do about his immediate financial problem? The matter occupied his thoughts as he stared vacantly at a young lady training in the ship's pool. Dunc noticed she had an elastic band around her waist that was attached to the end of the pool. He also noticed that she was 'stroking like Dawn Fraser so I said, "that's the girl for me"'. Dunc needed an athletic female type to help with a bright idea he had come up with. He was sure he knew how to raise the cash to get him comfortably home. The ship's notice board advertised a social activity involving horse racing. It promised cash prizes and interested parties were invited to apply to the purser. Upon further investigation, Pagey learned that the 'horses' were wooden equine images attached to a rope. As quickly as they could the competitors had to wind the rope around a spindle with the first home declared the winner. Dunc immediately noticed that if you reeled the horse in too quickly, the rope would tangle and if you went too slowly, well, that wasn't an option. Success required a steady hand. The race stipulated that a woman must work the spindle and reel the horses across the finish line (it was an era with zero feminist sensitivities). Duncan knew what was needed and his scouting mission for potential partners came to fruition at the pool.

He approached her. She liked the idea and agreed with Dunc's suggestion that they should engage in some preliminary practice. The purser agreed to let them have a play with the horses and the spindles. Page and partner wasted no time and trained diligently for a couple of hours each day before the big event. Soon they had the technique down pat and were finely tuned. Duncan was nothing if not canny. He had noticed that the advertisement mentioned the presence of bookies to take wagers on the competitors. Unfortunately, he was broke. That's true enough, and if he hadn't been in a cabin, he would also have been homeless. All the same he borrowed two dollars from one of his cabin mates and that princely sum bankrolled the betting plunge on himself and his new teammate.

Dunc 'invested' two bucks on the first race. There were six other horses, and the A Team won with little difficulty. The bookie had them at even money, so they now had four bucks in the kitty. The next race was the quarter-finals so they put up the four dollars and again came first. This time the odds were two to one so they were eight dollars to the good. The semi-finals came around and Pagey got fours. Without batting an eye, he 'put the lot on and we won again'. Now he was rolling in cash – to the tune of thirty-two dollars. All of a sudden, the world seemed a better place. The finals came around and the pressure was really on. Dunc could only get two to one but again he went all up and again they came out an easy winner. In racing vernacular, they 'won by panels' and the happy winners collected sixty-four dollars. He wisely trousered the two bucks owed to his cabin mate, but that still left him rolling in it – he had sixty-two dollars to get him home. He was flush with funds; and had he been so inclined, Pagey could have dined on caviar and champagne all the way to Sydney.

Just when it looked like there would be some financial breathing space, the purser played silly buggers. He announced that it is customary for the owners to race each other. That was fine with Duncan. He knew what he was doing and he was stone cold sober – unlike the majority of the other competitors. Problem was, the bookies were on to him by then and offered less even money. He won with a leg in the air (more racing vernacular) but only pocketed about eighty dollars altogether. That was fine with him; a win's a win. But then the bastard purser did another dirty. With a huge smile, he announced that it was customary for the winning owner to shout drinks at the bar. That occasioned an immediate stampede and Dunc looked on in dismay at the crowded bar. He knew he was done for when the first order was for champagne and a steady stream of bubbly was poured after that. It was a shambles. When the bludgers were finished, the barman presented him with a bill that amounted to eighty-four dollars. Duncan forked over eighty bucks and said, 'that's all I've got mate, you've cleaned me out'.

The next morning, he was back to scrounging soap and toothpaste. What bothers Pagey most about the episode is that he didn't even have enough cash left to buy his partner a drink. She watched from a distance while he handed over the money and then listened to his apology that there wasn't a brass razoo left. He also wonders if that was the reason he never laid eyes on her for the rest of the voyage. So there you are. Yet again things were crook in the financial affairs of Duncan Page, and they didn't get any better until he walked through the front door of his Blakehurst home where Cy and Jessie waited with open arms.

A few days out from Sydney, the matter of getting his swag full of ammunition through customs troubled Pagey's conscience. The niggle got worse once the ship docked and there was a loud knock on the door accompanied by one word – 'customs'. Dunc gave his overstuffed bag one last dubious look and reached for the handle. If the horse race episode started successfully and ended with disaster, this potential disaster ended with spectacular success. With some trepidation, Dunc opened the door only to be nearly knocked over in surprise. The officially attired customs officer gave Dunc a look of astonishment, collected himself and said, 'G'day mate, how ya goin'?' Unspoken prayers had been answered. When the customs officer turned out to be none other than a North Cronulla Surf Club mate, hands were shaken, backs slapped and then it was down to business. As his mate sized up the bag with the contraband ammo, Pagey confessed, 'I've got a problem. How am I going to get it through customs?' The customs officer gave him a wink and said, 'No worries mate'. He took a large yellow crayon from his left hand shirt pocket and placed a cross on the bag saying, 'There, now you just take it straight through customs'. Today Dunc shakes his head at the amazing coincidence, 'You know, I shot that ammo for years and years after that'. The legacy of Fort Sam and the inherent generosity of the people that welcomed him there lingered for years.

In no time he was home and back at work. 'I needed some brass to get over to England to catch up with Pete and Don.' Again, he went back to his small saddlery in the shed in the Blakehurst backyard. 'I found things just like I had left them a couple of years ago'. With typical industry he started working and saving for his next foreign expedition. Dunc specialised in small items – belts, gun holsters, rifle slings and so on. That was the mainstay of his working life and it continues to this very day. In three short months he had come up with the readies and was on his way, by plane this time, to London. The reunion with Pete and Don was tempered by the realisation that hungry days lay ahead while they represented their country in Europe. Slow starvation and penury – just part of the job for Australia's pentathletes.

18

THE COLD WAR

The Cold War was well and truly hot when the intrepid trio invaded Germany. Invasion is probably too strong a word. It was more like an underfunded and slightly chaotic summer holiday. Pete and Don, for reasons known only to themselves, wound up in the East German town of Bielefeld while Dunc, coming over from Australia, arrived where they should have been, in Bielefeld, West Germany. There were two such towns with that name – one east and one west. The western Bielefeld was home to the British troops stationed in Germany for the duration of the Cold War. The town was the headquarters for the fighting command known as the British Army on the Rhine (BAOR). The command was disbanded only after the Berlin Wall crumbled and the two Germanys reunited. The Pentathlon Three had come to the western version of Bielefeld because it was the training HQ for the Pommie pentathletes.

Pete and Don were party to a John Le Carré moment during their short sojourn as guests of the East German regime. Before long the boys were aware that their hosts had provided them with a 'tail'. In retrospect it was probably a Stasi agent assigned to shadow their every nefarious move. The bloke did his best to be unobtrusive but, in truth, he wasn't up to the job. Tired of the attention from their shadowy companion, Pete and Don decided to have some fun. They set off for a quiet stroll down a street until they came to an intersection. Suddenly Pete turned right while Don went left, leaving the spy catcher scratching his head. The poor bugger didn't know which way to turn and remained frozen to the spot until the boys circled back and walked up behind him. Not even Bond could have displayed more sangfroid as they nonchalantly strolled past him.

When the team finally assembled at the correct Bielefeld, the reunion was warm enough, but they found that their living conditions left a lot to be desired. No accommodation had been arranged for them but by now that was nothing new. The Aussies, courtesy of their heedless administrators, were earning an unwelcome but well-deserved reputation as the poor relations of Modern Pentathlon. 'We were known as bums. When we turned up for a competition we had nothing, so we just had to make do.' Other countries provided full on support for their pentathletes but the Aussies got bugger all. They were the absolute paupers of the sport. It was only the kindness of friends and acquaintances that helped them find a place to stay. They were couch surfers many years before the term was coined. 'We relied on word of mouth – "Try so and so, maybe he'll put you up for a while". We stayed wherever we could, lounges, floors, empty flats, you name it, we did it.' To make matters worse, Don was still suffering the after-effects of hepatitis and was battling it with long periods of sleep. The homeless caper in Bielefeld 'lasted only about a week' until the Brits found them an attic room in an old army barracks, and that became their home for the rest of their stay.

Travelling between the various destinations was a major operation. It wasn't as simple as showing up at the airport, weighing in your suitcase and Bob's your uncle. The well-equipped pentathlete was responsible for a lot of gear – there were saddles and fencing accoutrements, there were pistols and ammunition – things that were not commonplace for your ordinary traveller. The trick was to muster it into a coherent package at the beginning of the trip and trust it would arrive in the same condition at the destination. It was an exercise in logistics that most countries took care of for their competitors. But that didn't happen for the Aussies. In departure lounge after departure lounge, they stoically watched while harried customs officials dealt with borderline items like horsewhips and pistols. But somehow their gear would eventually arrive in one piece. Just as well because the Bielefeld attic dwellers needed it to prepare for the British Army on the Rhine (BAOR) Modern Pentathlon Championships.

If travel and accommodation were major hassles, food, and how to obtain it, was never far from their minds. The foraging expeditions that ensued were often the cause of merriment. Late at night in the Sergeant's mess, they discovered that the day's uneaten food was laid out on tables for passers-by to consume. One night, Dunc and Don crept in, turned on the light and prepared to attack the leftovers. Ravenous appetites were quashed in a heartbeat when the lights revealed that a table groaning with food was also blackened by thousands of cockroaches. The stomach-churning sight sent them back to bed, appetites unsatisfied. Peter, who had been elsewhere, came to bed in a particularly chirpy mood. He took great delight informing the boys that, 'You blokes don't know what you missed out on. You should have seen all the food in the Sergeant's mess.' Dunc and Don then took greater delight informing him about what they had seen earlier. No record exists of Peter's response but, for one night at least, the other two didn't object to the hollow sound of rumbling stomachs as they drifted off to sleep.

A similar episode of food thievery occurred later at Aldershot, a large military base in England. The base was host to a polo club and, on match days, a generous spread was laid out for the competitors. The boys chanced upon it while on one of their pilfering forays. The sumptuous repast, ever so daintily presented on paper doilies, waited expectantly for the competitors to finish. With zero compunction, the voracious antipodean raiders attacked the exquisitely displayed platters. Appetites sated, they were walking out the door just as the players returned to savour cucumber sandwiches, petit fours and Ceylon tea served in the finest china. Pagey laughs at the episode. 'The plates all looked like they had been nibbled at by mice. There were bits and pieces missing everywhere.'

There were occasional moments when food wasn't a pressing issue— but they were exceedingly rare. One such moment occurred when the boys were entertained at an extremely posh restaurant. Pete, Don and Dunc in a swanky restaurant at that time of their lives? It requires some explanation. Somewhere along the way they ran into a fellow Aussie who owned a used car dealership in town. The bloke was a West Australian who, once he came to know them better, informed them that he once had a bit of a reputation as a junior athlete. A bit of a reputation all right – as a junior he had beaten Herb Elliot in a mile race. Since no one had ever bested Herb in open competition, the car salesman immediately captured their attention. They started knocking around together and, after a while, the bloke asked if, as a favour, they would drive three used cars to Düsseldorf. The boys were happy to oblige, and the Herb conqueror promised to pay them handsomely. They politely declined the offer so he said he would shout them dinner at the best restaurant in town.

The offer of a slap-up meal was too good to refuse so the date was set. Pete and Dunc dressed for the occasion in their Australian blazers – the only good clothes they owned. The cuisine was spectacular. Dunc remembers that it was 'a real high-class meal'. He was mightily impressed by the opulent décor and the wandering gypsy band with a violinist who came right up to the table. Most of all he remembers the flambés igniting spectacularly and unexpectedly in all parts of the room. The boys hooked in and ate up big, thoroughly enjoying the brief respite from penury. Meal finished; their new mate told them to wait outside while he paid the bill. They wandered off, 'maybe two hundred yards up the street', when they saw their host putting in the big ones running toward them. 'Quick, jump in the car', he shouted. The boys were in the car in a flash while their host put the pedal to the metal. With some irony, and remembering his own sudden departure from Mexico City, Dunc says, 'I was deeply shocked'. The bloke had done a runner of course and, by way of explanation he told his passengers, 'I stood at the counter for a few minutes, but no one came. So I said, "Blow this, I'm out of here".' His guests, themselves in no position to comment on non-payment for services rendered, shared his amusement. To this day Dunc is concerned that the German diners might have noticed his and Pete's Aussie blazers.

The world championships in Mexico had clearly been a learning experience for the Pentathlon Three. The experience was salutary because, a year later, they struck a purple patch of form in England and Germany. In the BAOR Modern Pentathlon event Dunc came first in the individual championship. Along the way he set an Australian as well Commonwealth record in the shoot while performing close to his best in the other events. Peter maintained the momentum coming in a respectable sixth. It seems the German air was working wonders. All up they spent about three months at the Bielefeld base and then it was over to Aldershot for the British Army pentathlon championships. Aldershot, 'The home of the British Army', was a huge military base – bigger even, Dunc thinks, than Fort Sam. Now it was Peter's turn to shine, and he did just that. He finished second in the Pommie pentathlon championships while Dunc followed him into eighth place. But the weight of their initial success in Germany and then England couldn't be replicated when they crossed the Alps for the world championships in Bern, Switzerland. Dunc describes their performance there as 'just ordinary'. When asked why, after the promising start to their European campaign, his reply is succinct, 'We were all crook again mate'.

If food and accommodation were ever present problems, so too was failing health. In various ways the boys all suffered from malnutrition, and for a while their wellbeing was seriously compromised by boils that erupted all over their bodies. One morning Pete woke up to find Dunc inspecting a large boil that had surfaced on his backside. Pagey laughs when he admits that its location was unfortunate. It was hard to sit down on a chair, and harder still to sit on a horse. Things came to a head (if you will pardon the expression) when Pete was taken to hospital with malnutrition and a serious infection in his thumb. The World Championships in Bern were just around the corner and, after a few days of recuperation, Pagey and Don came to get their mate out of hospital. They found Peter comfortably ensconced in an easy chair, feet up on a pouffe and looking very pleased with himself. In fact, he was feeling much better now, except for the infection in his thumb – hospital food, atrocious though it may be, was better than no food at all. Pete's spirits were so high that he informed his mates that he intended to tarry a while longer. The other two cajoled and pleaded but Pete was adamant. 'What about the world championships mate?' 'Nope, I'm not going. I'm staying here.' 'What do you mean you're not going? You have to go.' 'We were ready to go to Bern, but not Pete. He wasn't shifting.' Eventually he relented but only after 'we dragged him out of his chair, got his gear together and put him on a bus. Then it was off to Switzerland.' Pete's infected thumb was lanced and the comfortable chair with its accompanying pouffe was reluctantly left behind. This situation was not exceptional, but what is incredible is the simple fact that through all the relentless adversity, the absolute commitment of the Pentathlon Three stayed rock solid. They never wavered in their commitment to representing their country. Today it stands as a beacon for all Australian sportspeople.

At various times over the years, all three men have related the following story with varying degrees of residual animosity. The Modern Pentathlon championships in Macolin (Bern) Switzerland may have been a world-class venue for competition but, for some reason, the athletes were expected to pay for their own food in the dining room. That wasn't a problem for competitors from countries that actually looked after them. Those fortunate dined gratis, but it was a big problem for the Aussies who, yet again, were quite literally standing on the bread line. What they were subjected to is almost inconceivable, but it is a simple fact that Duncan Page, Peter Macken and Don McMiken were reduced to waiting outside that Macolin dining room for Yanks and Brits to bring them leftovers. That was bad enough, but a bad situation got even worse when they spotted the only Australian Olympic representative at the championships gorging himself on fine Swiss cuisine while his countrymen scavenged for table scraps. The well-fed blazer never once graced them with his presence. Never inquired about their welfare. Never even brought them a sandwich. As Pagey says, 'He was there but he never bothered to say g'day'. The bloke was only sighted at the dinner table, and then only through a crack in the door. But given what is generally known about the Olympics, and the gilded treatment lavished on its administrators, one is hard-pressed to express surprise. The treatment of the boys was a national disgrace. How they maintained their resolve, in the face of deep neglect by officialdom, is one of life's great mysteries. The explanation which Dunc repeats for emphasis, 'We wanted to do it mate. We wanted to do it.'

Somewhere along the way Pagey struck up a friendship with one of the

East German pentathletes and they enjoyed several cordial conversations before and after training. Dunc learned that his new mate was a reserve for the team and expressed his commiserations. The German appreciated his new friend's condolences but brushed them off. He smiled broadly at the Aussie, spread his arms in an expansive gesture and said, 'Oh no, I have won. Look at my life here. This is where I am, and all those poor people at home are back there. I tell you this my friend, I have no regrets, for I have won.' That gave Dunc pause for reflection as he tried to stifle his rumbling stomach. The East German reserve could scoff all the food he wanted in the canteen while the Aussie mendicants huddled outside the door. It takes little to imagine the three of them, clad in tattered Australian track suits with bowls in hand addressing a bulging bellied blazer saying in piteous tones, 'Please sir, we want some more'.

The time they spent in Germany was not without an upside. In addition to Dunc's win in the BAOR championships and Peter's strong showing in the same event, they came across a man whose technical skill allowed them to improve their shooting significantly. The chap was an excellent gunsmith. Pagey was delighted to have discovered him. He knew exactly how he wanted his pistol to operate so it would fire more efficiently but had never found anyone who could put his ideas into practice. Not until he met this man in Bielefeld. The gunsmith, who was 'really great at his craft' made several minor alterations to the pistols which culminated in a major improvement to their handling. The gunsmith applied himself to 'accurising our firearms' (Pagey assures me it's the correct word). 'He skilfully polished and filed them until they were as light as possible.' Dunc reckons it resulted in a ten per cent improvement in his shooting. 'Ten per cent is a lot you know. Do the same thing with an ordinary Holden and you would turn it into a racing car. Well it was just like when he accurised our pistols.'

While on the subject of pistols, Dunc tells a story about Don's preference for his American Hi Standard 22 short. He and Pete were happy with their recently souped up Smith and Wesson K22s. Their firearms had the added advantage of using .22 long rifle ammunition which came in British Army issue cans containing 600 rounds. Every now and then one of the Brits would top up their supply with another can. On the other hand, because of his preference for the American firearm, Don needed a permit for his ammunition from the local constabulary. He duly fronted up at the police station, filled in the paperwork and received the permit. The ammunition came in a small box with a hundred rounds. It wasn't long before – the next day in fact – he ran through that, so it was back to the police station. The officer at the desk gave him a cool look and peremptorily denied his request. A less than impressed Don asked why and was told, 'Sorry lad, it looks like you've used up your year's supply then'.

The team's ordinary showing in Bern brought a dismal end to a campaign that had started with such promise. They arrived in Switzerland 'in good spirits' and Peter, after his enforced rest, felt well. Only in retrospect did Don and Duncan realise that they had trained far too hard. Their training regime was a matter of going flat out every day – in every event. He understands now that 'we were in a continual state of tiredness'. Even Peter, the only one who was properly rested, started feeling crook again. The one bright spot was Duncan's fine showing in the shoot where he came second. It was pretty obvious that the expertise of their German gunsmith was paying off big. But that one result was the best of a generally bad performance. Licking their wounds, it was time to go home and regather. The Tokyo Olympics loomed large on the horizon.

The Bern championships offered a couple of amusing incidents that Dunc enjoys retelling. The first involves a British competitor who was really a transplanted South African. Pagey says the bloke was a fair dinkum psychopath who was prone to sudden and violent rages. With much swagger and bravado, the bloke claimed that he was never nervous during the shoot. Dunc was a close witness to his nerveless performance during the Bern shoot. The South African/Pom was shooting a couple of bays down from Dunc when there was an unusual clack and clatter on the floor. Pagey looked over for the source of the sound and saw the bloke's dentures lying on the ground. The nerveless competitor's iron will had broken them in half.

Duncan and the now toothless competitor shared a mate – the British pentathlete, Jim Fox. Pagey describes Jim as a Michael Caine lookalike. He had a similar appeal to the ladies. 'Mate the birds were lining up for Jimmy. He could take his pick.' Dunc remembers him as a warm and engaging companion as well as an outstanding pentathlete who was a member of gold winning team at the Montreal Olympics in 1976. Dunc happily recounts the time Fox put in a less than gold medal performance in the ride at the BAOR competition. After the competitors finished their rides and had seen to their horses, they would congregate near the finish line to watch the others come in. The last jump at that competition was barely thirty yards from the finish so the onlookers had a fine view of Jim as he charged up on his grey horse. The clock was ticking and he urged on his mount at the final jump. Jim's horse had other ideas and flat out refused to have a go. The grey's sudden stop didn't halt its rider's momentum and Jim went flying over both horse and jump. He fell heavily but had the presence of mind to retain his grip on the reins. Jim tried to remount but the horse shied away, pulling the bridle off its head in the process. After loudly calling the animal every name he could think of, Jim somehow remounted and twice more approached the jump. By then he was hanging on the horse's ears and using them to guide it. Twice more the horse refused the jump. At the final refusal the clock had run out on him and Jim was mightily annoyed. He looked around, found the bridle and threw it at the horse. The horse thereupon elegantly surmounted the jump and cantered across the finish line. The other competitors who were watching Jim's travails, partly in sympathy and partly in amusement, responded with much laughter and much applause as the horse cantered past them.

Before hopping on a plane for the long journey home, Dunc took a couple of days to go up to Wakefield at the invitation of his mate Mike Hurst. There was a method in his madness – the Australian rugby league side was playing at Wakefield and Pagey was keen to see the game. Mike picked him up in his Austin A40 and off to the ground they went. After the game, Dunc caught up with a couple of the boys – the St George John's – Riley and Raper. He checked out their Australian blazers and couldn't help but notice that they were a dead spit for his Pentathlon World Championship blazer. 'Probably made in the same shop.' Dunc deliberately kept his overcoat buttoned up tight. 'I wasn't game to take off my overcoat in case they thought I was an imposter.' Yet another measure of the man's incredible inherent humility.

Pete and Dunc reconnected and headed home by way of Hong Kong. Don was going back to Oz but with a stopover in Mexico. Not the way most people would go but Don had his reasons. It seems that while he was a reserve at the World Championships Don had used his time wisely. A full year later and there he was, returning to reconnect with the lovely señorita who had caught his eye. Apparently, Dunc wasn't the only Aussie with an attraction to Mexican beauty. It so happens that this particular lady was the daughter of a famous Mexican picador – a picador is the guy who rides into the ring and goads the bull with a lance. Not only was this Mexican notably first-rate at his job, but he also owned an extensive hacienda set among Mexico's rolling brown hills. On this expansive property he selectively bred his country's premium fighting bulls.

Don was welcomed into this bucolic setting with open arms and he and his señorita got serious about getting serious. That was all well and good but, after a week or so, she informed Don that the coming Sunday was a very special day. It was the day the young bulls were to be tested. Only the best and the bravest make the grade. Each year the young men on the estate eagerly line up to test their courage by stepping into the ring and facing the bulls. Afterwards, the occasion would be celebrated with a grand fiesta. Don's potential father-in-law let it be known that his Australian guest was welcome to partake of this Mexican custom. It was a welcome that, to Don, sounded more like an unwelcome expectation. An expectation he had no intention of fulfilling. Put himself in front of a wild-eyed creature with lethal horns and snorting in rage? Señor Don didn't think so. That was never going to happen. Wisely he shot off to Qantas and booked the first flight out of Mexico. Much relieved, Don returned to the hacienda with that burden removed. It then became his melancholy duty to inform his picador-in-law that, while he appreciated the gracious hospitality, he had an urgent need to return home to Australia. So sorry, but he couldn't possibly linger. It was imperative to leave immediately. He deeply regretted missing the fiesta and the opportunity to test the bulls, but his flight was leaving the day before. Something similar must have been said to his dark-eyed señorita who would have responded with tearful understanding. Her fondest dreams were shattered; never would she applaud her gringo lover while he bravely faced the young bulls and their lethal horns. Departure day dawned and with no great reluctance, Don bade the raven-haired señorita a fond 'hasta la vista baby'.

19

KONNICHIWA TOKYO

It was a warm Sydney Christmas in 1963 when the world traveller finally returned to his family home. No sooner had he unpacked his bags than he was flat out 'working in the shed at the bottom of the backyard'. The cold, hard fact was he had to dig deep to pay for the privilege of representing his country. Recent experience clearly proved there would be no help forthcoming from the big shots in the Australian pentathlon association. So Pagey beavered away in his saddlery and worked even harder at his sport. Tokyo and the Olympics waited just around the corner and there were the trials before that. While the boys were away in Europe, Lloyd Mitchelson was making a name for himself by winning two Australian pentathlon championships. Lloyd's arrival on the scene was a spur to Pagey's determination to improve his performance. His form in the swim needed attention and, after a trial and error process involving a couple of coaches, he found his man in Terry Gathercole. In his time Terry had been a first-rate breaststroker and, when it came to coaching, he was the kind of man who knew his business. Dunc was encouraged because even though his bung leg wouldn't allow him to kick properly, he was sure he could improve his technique with Terry's help. Improved technique would result in better times and add points to his overall result.

Terry was just as pleased that the Pentathlon Three sought him out. In them, he knew he was dealing with mature and highly motivated athletes. It would make a welcome change from some of his younger protégés. Terry had a fine reputation as a coach – Ian O'Brien, the eventual gold medallist in the 200 metres breaststroke at Tokyo, was under his tutelage. On Ian's best day, Dunc remembers him as a reluctant trainer. So reluctant that Terry often showed up at his house to get him out of bed. 'Ian was just one of those naturals, but he was also the laziest person I've ever seen.' Today the correct term would be 'unmotivated' but, lazy or not, Ian O'Brien was never hampered by self-doubt. Before the Olympic breaststroke final Dunc stopped to offer Ian a quiet word of encouragement. Pagey wished him well and asked how he thought he would go. The laconic reply was, 'Oh she'll be right, I'm going to win. No risk.' Ian's genuinely unaffected self-confidence served him well. He came home with a gold medal as well as an Olympic and world record. Terry Gathercole, the master coach, never came near that level of success with the pentathlon boys, but their rock-solid work ethic certainly made his life easier.

Over the years, Dunc trained under other well-known Australian coaches and rates Terry as the pick of them. 'He was a really good fellow, Terry.' Pagey wasn't wrong. Once he came to understand the level of their commitment, the generous Gathercole told the boys he would like to coach them 'for free'. Terry's open-handed largesse stands in stark contrast to an earlier experience Dunc had with another giant of Australia's coaching ranks – Forbes Carlile. The great Forbes was himself a pentathlete who represented Australia at Helsinki in 1952. With that in mind, Pagey thought Carlile might be a natural fit. Rather diffidently, he approached the man at his Drummoyne pool. Forbes was speaking to another person, but he broke off the conversation and curtly asked what Dunc wanted. Pagey hastily explained himself and was told to get in the pool and do a four-forty warm up. Determined as always, Pagey did as instructed. When he finished, he climbed out of the pool and approached Forbes to ask what he wanted him to do next. Carlile, who was still involved in his conversation, said, 'All right, now I want you to swim a three hundred for time'. Back in the water Pagey went and did as directed. Swim finished; it was back to Forbes who was still deep in conversation. When Dunc politely asked for advice on how he could improve his swim time, the sage of the chlorine world advised, 'Son, you will improve your swimming by swimming more. Now please pay the lady at the gate two guineas.' In pre-decimal days a guinea was worth a pound and one shilling. Today it represents a fair whack to pay for advice that went something like, 'Mate, you can get better at swimming by swimming more. Now piss off and pay the lady as you go out the gate.' No wonder Terry's arrival was a breath of fresh air and, better still, his hand never went near Dunc's back pocket.

Peter was the first to adopt a smarter approach to his training regimen. Maybe his time in the hospital easy chair got him thinking about the need for occasionally having a lighter day. But the message hadn't filtered through to Pagey and Don. They continued to flog themselves – 'Each day we tried to beat our personal best from the day before'. It was a long time before they realised how counterproductive that was to their general performance. And that is where Terry Gathercole made such a big difference. He was the first to listen to them and recognise when they were knackered. He understood the need to lighten the training load from time to time. They didn't have carte blanche to ignore the program – Terry was a stickler for that – but when he saw that they were flagging, he didn't hesitate to lighten the load. It worked a treat because, at long last, Dunc's swim times were significantly improving. Despite Terry's humane approach, there was no absence of extremely hard days in the pool. After one gruelling session, Pagey drove home to find Cy, axe in hand, knocking over a tree in the front yard. 'Here Dad, give me that. I'll do it for you.' It was the natural and generous reaction of a responsible son. But as soon as he picked up the axe, Duncan knew he was stuffed, and said, 'Sorry Dad, I can't do it. I've to go and lie down.'

For the Pentathlon Three to maintain a steady training rhythm in the different disciplines they had to travel far and wide to the different venues. Not only did they train hard, they had to work just to make ends meet. It wasn't easy to keep things balanced and flowing harmoniously. The daily routine started first thing with the drive to Victoria Park, near Sydney University, to train with Terry. Then it was back to the day job. In the afternoons, it was over to the Sydney Pistol Club at La Perouse to have a shoot – Pagey delights in recalling that he never ran out of the purloined Fort Sam ammunition. In the evenings they went for a run at Centennial Park. Three nights a week after the run they trained at the Sydney Fencing Club at Rushcutters Bay near Kings Cross. There Dunc fenced and defeated three-time Australian champion, Ivan Lund – 'The best fencer Australia had'. He doubts that Ivan was at his absolute best and thinks the master may have been foxing – testing Dunc's ability for future reference, possibly in an Olympic trial. The ride – what about the ride? When asked that question, Pagey said that, in the absence of a nearby riding facility, they had to rely on their native ability and experience to get them through to the trials. Even for a person bereft of a comprehensive knowledge of Sydney and its suburbs, it is obvious that each day's training was a challenge. Not just in the training, but in the time-consuming distance travelled. Try fitting that in with your average day's work and it doesn't take long to realise that there weren't too many milliseconds left over for the ordinary things in life.

Time was of the essence, and the Olympic trials loomed large. Despite this, the Schweppes soft drink company thought the variety of action in Modern Pentathlon offered great opportunities for a TV commercial. The Olympic committee had no objections – as long as the money didn't go directly to the athletes – so they rolled the cameras. All five events were shown simultaneously on the screen and were broadcast throughout New South Wales. The commercial also showed up at movie theatres (Dunc first laid eyes on it at the drive-in). And the star of Schweppes' very own action movie was none other than Duncan Page. The star himself was too embarrassed to watch it because the saddle they made him use was a stock saddle and not a proper jumping saddle. Try as he might to avoid seeing himself on the big screen, the ad's exposure was so widespread that the inevitable happened. One night at a drive-in movie (the name of his lady companion is lost to antiquity) flashing across the screen was a larger than life action man who rode and shot and fenced and ran and swam in glorious split screen technicolour. Dunc tried to slink over to the kiosk to purchase something for his lady friend only to become acutely aware that people were staring at him – obviously mistaking him for someone famous. The question has to be asked – did Schweppes kick in anything to improve Pagey's financial wellbeing? What do you reckon? As an amateur sportsman in those days, he wasn't entitled to a brass razoo. The money went down the gaping maw of the Olympic fund, only to surface again when its big shot emissaries dined out in style.

UNSTOPPABLE

Three Olympic trials were scheduled before the Tokyo Olympics – two in Melbourne and one in Sydney. At the time, the southern city was the capital of Modern Pentathlon. The major decision makers lived there – big cheeses like Xavier O'Driscoll – and that's where the action was. With the approaching trials, time was getting short and nerves were twanging. The arrival of Lloyd Mitchelson as the new pretender added to the sense of urgency. It wasn't that Lloyd was a serious threat to anyone among the Pentathlon Three – as long as they performed up to expectations things would be fine. But the man's incessant carping and unrealistic expectations were a constant thorn in their side. It certainly didn't assuage Duncan's well-earned paranoia. All he wanted was to make the team and go to the Olympics. That always was, and remained, his prime ambition. It drove his competitive fires. But like other ambitions in his sporting past – the Olympic hurdles for instance, and let's not forget the twin fiascos at Wakefield-Trinity and St George – he had a healthy respect for the vagaries of Murphy's Law. Lloyd had won two Australian pentathlon championships in their absence and in his own mind that meant he was the rightful representative. Didn't matter who was listening, Lloyd wasn't backward about coming forward. His bragging earned him the nickname of 'Cassius' (for the younger generation: Cassius Clay was the birth name of Muhmmad Ali). Unfortunately, the 'greatest' version of Lloyd never quite got the pentathlon runs on the board. In the ten years of competing against each other, he got the better of Dunc once. That didn't stop Pagey from regarding the man an unwelcome distraction. Much as he tried to ignore him, as long as Lloyd's gums kept flapping, the 'whatever can go wrong, will go wrong' theory hung over Dunc like the Sword of Damocles.

Pagey improved his selection chances immensely by winning the Metropolitan Modern Pentathlon Championships in Sydney. Competitors came from all over Australia to take part, but it didn't matter who showed up that day because Dunc's hot streak in the shoot was glowing red. The German master craftsman's handiwork continued to do its thing and Dunc equalled the Australian record (curiously enough it was his own record set in Bielefeld) while winning the whole shebang. The thorn in his flesh, Lloyd Mitchelson, finished well back in the field, but that didn't stop his mouth from moving. Lloyd could never observe the aphorism, 'silence is golden'. As a measure of his verbal intemperance, it is instructive to consider an incident in his early days in the New South Wales police force. The young probationary constable sat at his desk attending to paperwork when a voice from behind said, 'You'd better get a proper haircut sonny'. Without looking up or, better still, thinking for a second, Lloyd retorted, 'You can't tell me what to do'. His reply was uttered without so much as a look at the officer walking past his desk. Had Constable Mitchelson not been so precipitate, he would have spotted the layers of braid on the distinguished officer's uniform. That might have led him to reconsider his manner of speaking. But Lloyd didn't do any of that, and his rash response failed to impress the Commissioner of Police. So unimpressed was the Commissioner that the probationary constable found himself immediately 'promoted' somewhere beyond the back of Bourke. If subsequent history is any guide, Lloyd's outback penance had little or no effect on his penchant for the verbal faux pas.

In the wash up of events, Dunc needn't have worried. He ran second in the trials – to Peter – and he was going to Tokyo. All the same, it was a considerable relief when he received the official letter informing him of his selection. He sat back and relaxed when they were on the plane to Japan. The flight was uneventful except for Lloyd's carping to anyone who would listen that he had been dudded to be a mere reserve. After all, wasn't he twice the Australian champion? The Pentathlon Three, especially the ever-sensitive Pagey, resented being badmouthed by Lloyd to their fellow Olympians, most of whom had probably never heard of Modern Pentathlon. Once the disaffected man ran out of people to listen, he put down his violin and only the normal low-level of discontent remained.

As you would expect from the host country, the Tokyo Olympics was organised to the nth degree. The village was scrupulously tidy and orderly. Every possible need was catered to, except one – space. Tokyo's dense population left the athletes with no room to move, no opportunity to limber up and properly stretch their legs. And for most that meant nothing more than going for a jog. But where to find a place to do that? In a park of course. Then they spotted it – a lovely park just outside the Olympic Village. Every mind of every athlete, from every country immediately thought as one. The park, which was not open to the public, was soon inundated with tracksuits. It was patrolled by two guards of shortish stature and they were no match for the largish athletes who descended on them. Despite the guard's earnest protestations, the park was taken over by men and women striding out as their bodies dictated. The athletes were answering their need to taper, and what better way than a light jog in a lovely park?

When the whips got cracking, the Aussie pentathletes showed solid form. Peter did 'exceptionally well' by finishing fourth in the individual standings. The team performance following on the back of Pete's success, did almost as well – coming fifth. Yet again the boys were able to compete at their best despite less than optimal circumstances. This time it was in the fencing competition where they were handicapped. It seems they had to make do with just two épées between the three of them. In consequence none of them had use of an épée that was for their own personal use –an épée they knew well and were accustomed to using. Two épées between three blokes? Bit of a joke that, especially when the Hungarians, who took out the team honours, were given an unlimited number of épées to choose from. Dunc goes on to mention another oddity of the Tokyo competition – the ride. For the first time ever, seventy-five per cent of the horses had a clear round (they didn't miss a jump). That level of success was unheard of, and Dunc says that 'the calibre of the horses was far too good for the calibre of the course'. In consequence, the better riders like him were disadvantaged. It meant that he couldn't expect to pick up the points in the ride he was certain to lose in the run.

Don had an interesting experience finishing the ride – if 'interesting' means being disqualified. Don was accused of dismounting from his horse before being given permission to do so. That was not the done thing in the pentathlon ride. The disqualification got him justifiably fired up, so he protested the decision. The Japanese handler, who had control of Don's mount, started speaking in a burst of his native tongue. The rider was perfectly fluent in English, although far from it in Japanese, took the handler's words to mean he was permitted to dismount. So he did. That was a big no-no. Whatever the handler had said, it wasn't, 'Righty-o mate, you can get off now'. An indignant Don protested vigorously to the rules committee (there is always a committee). The learned individuals deliberated at length after the disqualified rider had explained himself. In the end they rescinded the disqualification on the grounds that, in Pagey's words, 'Don wasn't to know what the handler was saying to him'. It seems that somewhere in the arcane list of do's and don'ts of Olympic competition the officials found a rule that stipulates all instructions must be given in either English or French. Don McMiken, who has never been one to back down, was ultimately vindicated. Unfortunately for him the contretemps in Japan wasn't to be his last encounter with boneheaded officialdom.

Dunc was less than thrilled with his individual result, but his disappointment was tempered by a night out with an enchanting local lass. Somewhere along the way he caught the eye of a lovely young lady – a young Japanese tennis player. The boys had been introduced to the Japanese junior tennis team and one of the female members took a shine to Pagey. The upshot of this instant attraction was that she 'invited me home for dinner'. Fortunately for all concerned the lass had a grandfather who, after having studied at the US Naval Academy at Annapolis, was fluent in English. It turns out he had worked on the Japanese midget submarine program before the war and probably had a hand in the incursion into Sydney Harbour that a much younger Pagey watched from his auntie's Kogarah veranda. The evening was fully chaperoned (a la Maria Elena in Mexico City) and Dunc recalls the experience as being less than satisfying. It was a standard Japanese house, which meant standard Japanese dining arrangements which involved sitting on the floor. Dunc couldn't bend his crook leg sufficiently to accommodate the low table. All evening long he shifted it in a vain attempt to find a less awkward position. 'The most uncomfortable meal I ever had.' He had been driven to his host's house but was put on a train for the return journey. The train let him off right outside the village – easy as. Dunc chuckles when he remembers how he was able to see clearly to both ends of the carriage by looking over the tops of the passenger's heads. Not something he was able to do on a Sydney train.

Not long after they finished their competition, and along with a fair swag of the other Aussie athletes, the Pentathlon Three were herded aboard a Qantas flight and unceremoniously shipped home. The early departure was as unexpected as it was unwelcome. Hadn't the airline flown the entire Olympic team to Tokyo as a single entity? That it had, but for some reason flying them back together proved impossible. The upshot? Many of the athletes who proudly marched into the Olympic Stadium during the opening ceremony missed out on marching in the closing ceremony. It is an absurdity to learn that Dunc vividly remembers downing tools in his shed to race inside to watch the closing ceremony on television with his mum and dad. As a matter of public interest, one would like to know how many non-competing Australian Olympic officials stayed behind to watch the closing ceremony in the stadium. Would it be a surprise to discover that they all stayed behind? No? Me either.

Before saying 'sayonara' to Japan altogether it is worth including a final anecdote – something Pagey recently related, almost as an afterthought. One day while at the training track in the Olympic Village Dunc noticed an African American athlete jogging steadily among the others similarly engaged. This bloke, obviously a boxer, was noticeable because he was attired in a white tracksuit and hood. That alone would have made him stand out from the crowd, but Dunc was struck by the intimidating expression on the man's face. 'There goes the meanest man I've seen here. I thought, "Whoever is going to fight him is in big trouble". He looked like he would tear you apart.' And the man under the white hood was? The Tokyo heavyweight gold medallist and later heavyweight champion of the world – the nemesis of Muhammad Ali – none other than Smokin' Joe Frasier. So there you go. Without realising it,

Duncan Page was hobnobbing with sports royalty.

20

MING THE MERCILESS

A week after returning from Tokyo Pagey was full of beans and ready to go. 'I was jumping out of my skin'. The pressure was off, he was feeling great and hard at work making a quid. The boys resisted the temptation to slack off and trained on as if the '68 Olympics in Mexico were next month and not four years away. Dunc is at pains to stress that, while the effort they put in could be exhausting, it was never a burden. There was always something or someone to lighten the load – and the lightening regularly came in the form of humour. 'The thing I most remember about our years together was the laughter. We laughed at almost anything – other people's misfortune as well as our own.' Always serious about their work, the Pentathlon Three refused to be miserable while they went about it.

There were inevitable changes in coaching personnel during the interregnum between the Tokyo and Mexico games. Coaches moved on, training procedures were tweaked, but the intensity never lessened. At their evening Centennial Park runs, they teamed up with Keith Ollerenshaw, the marathon runner who represented Australia at the Melbourne Olympics. Keith looked after their running schedules for a couple of years but when Al Lawrence returned from Houston they gravitated to him. Whenever Dunc reminisces about the good times in those years, the name of Al Lawrence constantly pops up. 'A lot of us fellows trained together at Centennial Park. There was no particular system or sophistication. It was pretty much catch-as-catch-can, but I really enjoyed the training. We seemed to laugh all the time. Al was always there cracking jokes.' When he took on the coaching responsibilities, Al became all business. In later years he went on to have a remarkable coaching career at the University of Houston. With the work he gave them at Centennial Park, the Pentathlon Three may very well have been Al's first crash test dummies. While Al had high expectations of his men, and he could be a hard taskmaster, he alleviated that with his irreverent sense of humour and the good times they shared.

As often happens in areas of human endeavour, there is a great divide in certain disciplines. There certainly is in the world of track athletes. The divide is demarcated in the line that is drawn between distance runners and sprinters. The former regard themselves as the hard workers of the track hierarchy and disdain the latter because of the brief time they are asked to expend maximum effort. Dunc recalls Al Lawrence spelling it out one evening. After he got back from Houston, Al played host to a group of American track athletes. Genial as ever, he showed them the sights of Sydney and then took them to Maroubra Beach for a body surf. Sprinter and distance runner alike frolicked happily in the shore break. Everyone was having a splendid time until one of the Yanks managed to be stung by a blue bottle. The poor bloke carried on as if he had lost a limb. Al, ever the considerate host, expressed concern. That was allayed when he was reassured by one of the injured blokes teammates – a distance runner – who drily commented, 'Don't worry about him Al, he's a sprinter and everyone knows they can't stand pain'. That explained everything in a language that only the long-distance runner can fully appreciate.

In Keith Ollerenshaw and Al Lawrence, the boys running needs were well looked after. That was a decided plus, but there was a much bigger and far less positive change when it came to the swim. Terry Gathercole, the man who prepared them for Tokyo, gave up coaching at Victoria Park in favour of a pool closer to home in North Sydney. That was quite literally a bridge too far for the Pentathlon Three. They were already chasing their tails all over town just to get to the various training venues and crossing the Sydney Harbour Bridge first thing every morning wasn't on the cards. Not when the return trip meant driving through rush hour traffic. With reluctance Dunc said goodbye to Terry and hello to Don Talbot.

In the Australian swimming world, Don Talbot stands as a colossus. His coaching career first came to the fore when he worked with John and Ilsa Konrads. Talbot's career never seemed to lose its upward trajectory. He was appointed Canada's national coach and, later, Australia's major domo, where he presided over a golden period culminating in the epic medal tally at the Sydney Olympics in 2000. Dunc approached Talbot in 1966 with a view to preparing for the '68 games. Terry Gathercole, the patient listener, was swapped for a martinet, more accustomed to dictating to young swimmers. Talbot either didn't know how or couldn't be bothered to understand the needs of a mature adult. The relationship was always going to end in tears, and sure enough it did. Even allowing for the generation gap between his usual clientele and the mature pentathlete, Talbot's approach to Duncan seems excessive.

The Pentathlon Three were the far from dilettantes or slackers. Each and every day the boys trained ridiculously hard in the component elements of their sport. There was also the factor of the time and distance spent travelling to the different venues. They then had to add that to their work commitments which funded their sporting activities and put food on the table. It wasn't as if the morning swim was the only thing on their daily schedule. The tunnel-visioned Talbot didn't see it that way. Dunc angrily retells one significant episode with him that set his wellbeing back for almost a year. Pagey showed up for training one morning without having fully recovered from his run the night before. Al Lawrence had set the boys a fifteen-mile time trial around Centennial Park. A time trial is exactly what it says – the athlete is required to expend maximum effort to make the required time. Pagey ran himself ragged to make the time. After that energy sapping effort, the boys hopped into their cars and drove to Rushcutters Bay where they fenced until just before midnight. Then it was home to bed and get up again for swim training at 6:00 am. Dedication and commitment to the pentathlon cause was a constant in their lives.

Unfortunately for the nearly exhausted mature age swimmer, Talbot was a one-trick pony. His coaching technique was 'one size fits all'. What worked for kids would work for adults. It was Pagey's bad luck that it didn't work for him and the inappropriate methods were disastrous. The morning after the fifteen-mile time trial and the late night fencing training, Pagey fronted up to the Hurstville indoor pool at the mandatory 6:00 am. No exceptions were allowed.

MING THE MERCILESS

Latecomers were peremptorily sent home. It started out as a normal session with Talbot overseeing Dunc and a group of kids. When they finished Talbot felt that none of them had given him an acceptable effort. His words were, 'I don't think you've been putting out. I want you to swim four fifty metre sprints and I want them done flat chat. I want a hundred per cent effort.' His rev-up was little more than the bog-standard mind games played by coaches in that era. But the man who got to bed at 12:00 am the night before had been 'putting out' – he always did. Despite misgivings, he wearily complied. First demand met; Talbot issued another. Using the same accusation, he sent them out to repeat their effort. That done, Dunc heard same words again, only this time reduced to 'swim another two'. The swimmers complied and then it was swim one more and it is 'definitely the last'. But it wasn't – Talbot had them swim one more. The man who was also known as 'Ming the Merciless' finally relented and let them get out of the pool. A bit hard that – the getting out of the water bit. By the end of that session Pagey could barely hang on to the edge. When Dunc staggered out, he knew one thing for sure – that would be the last of Don Talbot and his punitive coaching psychology.

With the benefit of hindsight Dunc now accepts that he and Talbot were never a good fit. He laments working with the man for the better part of half a year before dissolving the arrangement. 'He was used to dealing with kids and I don't think he realised that when you asked someone like me for a hundred per cent effort, that's what you got. You couldn't tell him when you were tired. He wouldn't listen. It was always "there's the program and that's it".' Pagey acknowledges Talbot's major successes with his younger protégés but, in his dealings with the man, he 'found him arrogant'. With more than a trace of residual bitterness, he has said more than once that 'you couldn't talk to him'.

Dunc never went back after Ming flogged the daylights out of him. Worse still, the after-effects of that twenty-four-hour period of intense work set back his general wellbeing for the better part of a year. For months after, 'I had no fight and my times went back terribly'. The pity is that the damage was completely avoidable. Talbot didn't seem to know or care that he was dealing with an Olympic athlete and couldn't see that his input was just one part of a bigger picture. As far as the boys were concerned, a swimming coach wasn't the major player in their scenario, there were lots of competing demands on their time and energy. Talbot may have been number one to the other swimmers – to Dunc he was just another coach. To this day Pagey expresses genuine resentment that, in the long weeks after Ming had been merciless, he was continually drained of energy – even at work in his shed. 'He didn't care that I also had to make a crust as well as train. I had to go to work every day and meet the demands of my customers.'

Pagey's backyard empire was humming along very well. He was flat out making leather goods for the likes of Mick Smith, the prominent gun dealer whose shop on George Street was something of a Sydney institution. He had started out as a barber who sold ammunition on the side, until what had been a sideline became the main line. Mick put down the clippers and set up a gun shop. Dunc remembers at one time, in the glory days, there were six gun shops dotted along George Street. Pagey came to know Mick well over the years and, if the recently deposed swim coach was an uncaring tyrant, the gun merchant could be generous and understanding. Modern Pentathlon challenged its competitors not only in terms of training requirements but also financially. The sport required constant outgoing expenditure. Dunc constantly chased his financial tail and was perpetually broke. The money from his business did little more than keep his head above water, and this is where Mick Smith occasionally entered the picture. The two men came to know each other well and Mick appreciated the quality of Dunc's saddlery work. He also understood and sympathised with his struggles with money. In his day, Mick had been a champion skeet shooter and was impressed by Pagey's deep knowledge of firearms. At times he could be a hard man in his dealings with customers, as Dunc often saw first-hand. 'He could be cantankerous, old Mick. I've seen him toss people out of his shop.' But when it came to helping out a mate, the irascible gun dealer was happy to 'slip us ammunition now and then'. Us? Always unselfish, Dunc happily shared Mick's largesse with Peter and Don.

MING THE MERCILESS

Once during a lean patch, the gun dealer came to Dunc's rescue. Pagey had a watch he was particularly fond of and, during a dry spell, he was thinking about off-loading it. He happened to be in Mick's shop and, on the spur of the moment, asked how much he would give him for it. Mick Smith was nothing if not canny. He answered the question with another. 'How much do you want for it?' Dunc considered the watch and then considered his answer. 'Five hundred dollars would be about right.' The businessman in Mick Smith came out in his response, 'This isn't a pawn shop mate'. Dunc's thoughts went something like, 'Oh well, it was worth a try'. Then, in the next breath, he heard Mick quietly instruct one of the shop assistants to take five hundred dollars out of the till. 'Give the money to Duncan, he'll fix us up when he can.'

If there were times when Pagey and the boys did it hard, there were always compensations. There was the laughter, the camaraderie and the generous kindness of people like Mick Smith to lighten the load. First among the compensations was the laughter. Ah, the ever-present laughter. With Al Lawrence as their coach, a good laugh was never far away, especially with his unlimited store of tales and yarns from his many escapades. There is one that must be shared because Dunc has repeated it several times and he says that Al told him it at least twice. It involves Al, the marathon at Rome, a Canadian marathoner and a goatskin of plonk. But before we get on to that, we have to go to England, and Al's supposed two-week hiatus from training before the Rome Olympics.

The standing rule for all Australian athletes living and competing overseas stated that to represent their country at the Olympics they had to return home and earn their place at the trials. Somehow the rule was bent to accommodate Al Lawrence before the 1960 games. After all, hadn't he gone undefeated for two years in races involving distances of two, three and six miles (as well as their metric equivalents)? Did he not hold world records in several of those distances? Al, who fully expected to have to return to Oz from Houston, was delighted at the let-off. He promptly took the opportunity to go to England for a couple of weeks before resuming training for Rome. That was the plan.

But when he got there, he felt so good he decided to train on. Better still, the harder he trained the better he felt. He couldn't wait to get to Rome.

The best-laid plans . . . Al hadn't accounted for the disparity between the mild English weather and the energy-sapping reality of mid-summer Rome. Pagey, there as an onlooker, remembers it being 'a hundred degrees outside every day'. No doubt the Flying Milko would have given the Olympic officials some for scheduling distance runs on baking Italian days. But Dave Stephens wasn't there, and Al was. He decided to have a run in the 5000 metres as a tune-up for the longer events later. It didn't go well. Halfway into the run Al 'was gone; he knew he was absolutely exhausted' and finished well back. He was so depleted after the race that he took a few days off to rest. He was getting himself ready for the marathon. Here is Al Lawrence's self-deprecating account of his 'exceptional' performance in the Rome marathon, as told to Duncan Page among others.

The temperature in Rome was brutal – a hundred degrees and counting. Doesn't matter how hot; the show must go on. Al started well and for the first thirty or so kilometres he ran easily and felt good. Alas, somewhere after that things went pear-shaped. The heat took its toll and Al 'got the staggers'. He went from running to jogging and then to walking. It got so bad that he sat on the kerb and, at last, he stretched out in the gutter. He lay there immobile for a couple of minutes and, when he opened his eyes, there was a bloke standing over him. The Italian fellow looked concerned and gestured to the large wineskin in his hand. The sign language said, 'Here mate, do you want some of this?' Al sat up and gratefully rehydrated on plonk. He was seriously thirsty, so he didn't hold back. Soon enough he was feeling okay and stood up gingerly. When he did that, Al realised he was 'as full as a boot'. There was nothing to do but start jogging and, as he looked around, he could see that like him, many other competitors were seriously exhausted. In an altered mind state, Al ran up behind the others and whacked them on the backside saying, 'Come on mate, let's get going'. With about a thousand metres to go he teamed up with a Canadian marathoner and they ran stride for stride until they came to the final stadium lap. The Canuck looked at Al and said, 'Do you want to sprint?' The response? 'No way, mate!' The Aussie then asked his new mate, 'Do you want to sprint?' Same response. So they linked arms in a fine gesture of Commonwealth solidarity and crossed the finish line to be recorded in joint forty-sixth position in the Rome marathon.

The boys loved Al's tall but true yarns and they enjoyed the follow up to his marathon story. After the run he was taken immediately to hospital where rehydration came from a drip rather than a goatskin. Al was an immensely popular member of the track team and a number of the others decided to pay him a visit. In one of the hospital corridors they came upon a Coca Cola dispensing machine – the old-fashioned chest type as opposed to the modern upright version. They unplugged it and thoughtfully carried it to Al's room where it was installed beside his bed. After paying their respects they left him to recuperate. All through that dark night in the quiet hospital in Rome, whenever the urge came upon him, Al reached out and satisfied himself with another icy cold bottle of Coke. Something similar happened to Peter Macken when he finished the Modern Pentathlon cross-country run. He too was seriously heat stressed. This time, Dunc remembers, had the ambulance taking Pete back to the village, not to the hospital. Different standards of care seem to apply to world record holders as opposed to great pentathletes.

One thing was for sure, when it came to running coaches, the Pentathlon Three were well served by their mate. Whenever Al Lawrence asked something of them, he was never asking anything he hadn't done himself many times over. With all the knowledge and expertise of a world-class athlete and coach, as well as great dollops of good humour, the boys knew they were on a winner.

21

LOOSE CHANGE

The group of runners that regularly congregated at Centennial Park in the evenings contained an eclectic mix of interesting characters ranging from the Kingsgrove Slasher to champions like Keith Ollerenshaw, Pat Clohessy and Al Lawrence. The tales and yarns of their successes and mishaps – and the laughter that came with them – were given a welcome air at Centennial Park. The stories never seemed to stop. Pagey enjoys retelling them and admits that the self-deprecating humour went a long way to easing the load. Looking back on those happy times he says that 'when you're fit and relatively young, life's a breeze'. But life was moving quickly. It was well into 1966, and the Melbourne world championships were at hand. A solid performance would go a long way to determining selections in the team for the '68 Mexico Olympics. Yet again the Pentathlon Three made the long drive south and got down to business. The rest of the pentathlon world was ready and waiting for them.

At the Melbourne championships, as always, the ride was the most problematic. Dunc drew a horse he had never heard of. Fortunately for him, he tracked down its owner. In response to the question, 'How does it go?', the woman replied, 'He's a great horse but no one can get him to jump over water'. Pagey's heart sank because there was a nasty water jump smack dab in the middle of the course. His first thoughts were something like, 'If the owner can't get him over water then I'm going to have some strife'. And sure enough, he did. The horse went smoothly around the course until it spotted the water and decided 'it was not going near it'. The inevitable happened. After one refusal, Dunc backed off and had another crack, saying to the horse, 'Mate, I'm going over it, I don't know about you'. He geed his mount up and when they came to the jump, 'I dug my spurs in hard and wound up on the horse's neck'. Somehow, the horse balanced itself and, while Dunc slid back onto the saddle, they cleared the jump. The time lost in the refusal resulted in an 'ordinary' performance. But he wasn't Robinson Crusoe because both Peter and Don had difficult rides. Despite a fine second placing in the shoot, Pagey rated the team's overall performance in Melbourne as 'very average'.

The individual winners came from Hungary and the Soviet Union. The team winners, in order, were Hungary, USSR and East Germany. All countries, for propaganda purposes, provided solid backing for their athletes. The disparity between Australia and the countries that supported their pentathletes was never more starkly evident. It was there for all to see – freshly minted in gold, silver and bronze. In Melbourne, the Aussies were no better off than they were in Tokyo. They could still muster no more than two épées between them. Two years had elapsed since the Olympics and the Modern Pentathlon Association still hadn't provided them with a third. Dunc acknowledges that épées were an expensive item and it was common to break them. But still – two épées between three men representing their country? Not good enough, blazers.

The role of Xavier O'Driscoll, who played a less than creditable part after the Melbourne championships concluded, comes into question at this point. What was his purpose if the athletes he represented regularly went without essential equipment? The boys deliberately had as little as possible to do with him, and for good reason. When asked if they ever approached the man for assistance, Pagey laughs and says, 'There was no way we could do that. You couldn't talk to the man.' Don McMiken didn't appreciate O'Driscoll's attitude to the athletes and wasn't afraid to show it. 'To him we were underlings. We were just peons.' Dunc agrees and says he was 'a contemptuous sort of man. He may have done good things for pentathlon but we, as competitors, never heard about anything he did. Nothing ever came back to the troops.'

Similar bureaucratic obstructionism arose between the pentathlon boys and the Australian Fencing Federation. Dunc remembers coming third in the Australian Fencing Championships in Brisbane but insists that he won the event. The judges, all from the association, saw it differently. Pagey may have a point when he says there was a suggestion of bias. He was an unaccountable omission when they were selecting the fencing team for the Commonwealth Games in Jamaica. The team comprised three athletes in the foils and three in the sabre, as was the customary practice. For some reason the association, in its wisdom, selected only two athletes to compete in the épée – Dunc's chosen event. After all, had he not come third? The Pentathlon Three got the impression that they weren't 'the flavour of the day' as far as the Fencing Federation was concerned. 'We were too rough and ready, not genteel enough. We weren't part of the inner fencing elite'. Indeed, one member of the Aussie fencing team, a chap named Bill Ronald – 'A man with a good opinion of himself' – openly stated that the pentathlon fencers were 'rubbish' and 'too rough'. With some satisfaction, Pagey remembers how Peter went on to clean up Ronald and his high opinion in the NSW State Championships in Sydney. Ill-will was forgotten a few years later when the fencing association selected Pete and Dunc in the épée team for the Mexico Olympics, where the 'rubbish' and 'too rough' members convincingly outperformed the more genteel Ronald.

Frustrations and niggles were inevitable when administrative ineptitude was concealed behind a veil of haughty condescension. Infuriating as they could be, these bureaucratic bungles were sometimes counterbalanced by bizarre moments of great amusement. At the Melbourne World Championships, the athletes were quartered in a national park near the city. Dunc can't recall its name or location – he was focused on the job at hand. Wherever it was located, the Soviet pentathlon team was training at the nearby shooting facility situated in a clearing among thick native forest. Also habituating the bush were resident bellbirds whose calls were clearly heard between shots. Dunc recalls how the Russkis would fire four rounds at their targets and then, 'just for fun', send the last round into the bush hoping to ping off one of the irritating bellbirds. In fairness to the Commos, they were living in a far less ecologically aware age.

On the day of the shooting competition, Pete and Dunc had no idea how to find the venue. They were advised by an official to follow the Soviet consular vehicle provided to ferry its athletes to the competition. The well-intentioned official failed to consider the small matter of diplomatic immunity. The consular car set off at a torrid pace, leaving the Aussie duo with no option but to ignore local speed restrictions in the effort to keep up. They knew they would be cactus if they lost the Soviet vehicle. It was pedal to the metal or they would be adrift in the vast expanse of suburban Melbourne. And then – it just had to happen – Pagey, who was behind the wheel, was pulled over by Victoria's finest. In his best cop-speak the officer asked, 'Are you aware that you were exceeding the speed limit, driver?' Of course he bloody well was. How else was he going to keep up with the flaming Russians? That was thought rather than spoken. The actual response was far more diplomatic. The arresting officer listened to Dunc's harried explanation and replied, 'Very well, then. You'd better follow me.' With lights flashing and siren wailing, the officer led them the ten miles or so to the shooting venue. He led them right up to the door. Then, with a wave and a 'Good luck boys', he turned around and took off.

Then there is the matter of the great double bunger purchase. By now they are probably extinct, but in its time the double bunger was a large firecracker with twice the normal punch of its smaller relations. On their way to Melbourne, Dunc and Pete stopped to look around a small country town in Victoria. They happened upon a small hardware store and, with much glee, pointed to what was prominently on display in the window. Right before their eyes was a large box of double bungers left over from cracker night. The boys sauntered in and bought the lot. They were certain that their purchase would prove useful later– and not just in Melbourne. 'We thought we'd have a bit of fun with them.' Was it mentioned that Peter Macken was a member in good standing of the New South Wales police force? No? Well, it is a fact worth remembering as this chapter progresses.

It didn't take long for the 'bit of fun' to materialise. While idling their time in the athlete's quarters one night, the boys walked past the Pommie room where the inhabitants were raucously enjoying a game of cards. Dunc couldn't help himself. He opened the door a couple of inches and rolled the massive double bunger under the table where it came to rest among the feet of the card players. In a matter of seconds, the firework did its thing. When asked about the reaction of the Brits, Pagey said, 'I wasn't there to see what happened, I'd shot through mate. But I heard the shouts and the swearing.' But disturbing the recreational activities of their Commonwealth brethren was just the beginning. They went looking to create more havoc. The Soviet team happened to be walking down the corridor and after they went past, the boys lit another bunger. This one went off at its usual startling decibel level. Soviet feet left the ground and Soviet heads hit the ceiling. At the other end of the hall was a Norwegian pentathlete innocently walking toward them. The Commos immediately suspected a Western capitalist plot. In retribution, they grabbed the Norse bloke and dragged him under the shower fully clothed. They were so busily engaged in exacting retribution that they failed to hear the click of the Aussies door as it ever so gently closed. There is more to come from the double bungers, but that must wait until they resurface in Mexico a couple of years later.

The championships ended with the boys less than satisfied with their middle of the pack result. Don flew out to New Zealand while the other two headed up the Hume Highway in Dunc's Morris Minor ute. When chided about owning a Morris Minor, rather defensively he says, 'I drove it everywhere'. As testament to its reliability, the best he can say is, 'Well, it never blew up on me'. In any event, he and Peter were about fifty miles south of Goulburn heading for the comforts of home. They came upon a couple of hitchhiking teenagers in possession of a large suitcase. Pagey pulled over and told them to jump into the back of the ute. You wouldn't do it today, but those were kinder times. The Morris, despite its greater load, was up to the job and motored on. A few miles up the road Dunc noticed a car following closely, then a car overtaking and, finally, a car forcing them off the road. They came to a full stop with Duncan thinking, 'Hello, these blokes are in cahoots with the blokes in the back'.

The suspected hijacking ended very quickly. Pagey just happened to have his firearm handy – it was never far away. Peter jumped out, with pistol and warrant card in hand, saying in his best copper voice 'New South Wales police, state your business'. Dunc laughs and says that the blokes who had forced them off the road nearly shat themselves. Their hasty explanation came out in a jumble of words. They had thought Pete and Dunc were helping the blokes in the back of the ute. It seems that the young fellows had helped themselves to the tools from a petrol station further down the Hume. A quick check of their suitcase revealed the true state of play. With that sorted out there was still the matter of accounting for the trainee crims. Peter, who abhorred the very idea of paperwork, advised the pursuers to take the young offenders directly to Goulburn Police Station. In a classic flick pass he assured them that the officers in that town were best placed to deal with the matter. Pete then jumped back in the Morris and said to Dunc, 'Come on, let's get out of here'.

After Melbourne, Don went in a completely different direction. He was flying to New Zealand to reconnect with the lovely Joy, the lady who was to become his wife. How he got there is another matter, so prepare yourself for what must stand as the most disgusting treatment ever handed out to an Australian international athlete. Yet again the spectral figure of Judge John Xavier O'Driscoll looms large. Prior to the Melbourne world championships, the lofty pentathlon poobah assured Don that he would be provided with the airfare to return to New Zealand. The post-championship function was held in a large shed. Think of the venue for a country barn dance and you're getting close. The hospitality was warm and the bar was well patronised – pay as you go, of course. O'Driscoll supervised the festivities and, as each of the boys will tell you, his hip flask was never far away.

Amidst the general revelry, things took a nasty turn when Don approached O'Driscoll. In a reasonable tone, he said, 'Look, I need the money you promised, I've got to catch a plane to New Zealand'. There was a history of bad blood between administrator and athlete. Don didn't like being told what to do by a person he regarded as an arrogant prick, and O'Driscoll didn't like being importuned by a lowly athlete. The Judge's response to Don's voice of reason may well have been fuelled by the consumption of spirituous beverages. Whatever the excuse, his subsequent response was inexcusable. In a towering rage, as inexplicable as it was titanic, O'Driscoll went to the bar's till and scooped up a handful of silver. He then threw it on the floor saying, 'There's your money, pick it up'. Don fixed the man with a steely look and did just that. The coins he scrabbled up were nowhere near enough to pay his way to New Zealand, but Don had had enough. Peter and Dunc were witness to O'Driscoll's tantrum and neither has forgotten the appalling episode. They often retell the incident because it speaks volumes about the administration of Modern Pentathlon in the sixties. Unpardonable and unforgiveable. A disgrace to Australian sport.

It was only the strength of their commitment that got them past the rough patches, even when confronted by the depths plumbed by Xavier O'Driscoll. The strength of that commitment was never more evident than on one fine Christmas Day in New Zealand. Don was celebrating the occasion with Joy at her parents' home and things were well in hand. Joy's mum reminded her that Christmas dinner would be served at the usual time around two o'clock. Joy gently explained that it wouldn't work for Don because he went for his run every day at that time. Mother laughed and thought her daughter was having a lend. She then went about her work thinking, 'Surely he will make an exception for Christmas Day'. The mother-in-law didn't know the measure of the man because at two o'clock sharp, just as the family sat down for the festive fare, out came Don in his running gear. Then it was out the door to hack a track. After all, the Mexico Olympics were just up the road.

There is a delicious epilogue to the ongoing friction between O'Driscoll and the athletes he considered unruly underlings. Athletes have a habit of retiring and when they retire, they see little need to toe the company line. There is no one to deny them selection. No one to blight their lives with incomprehensible decisions. Duncan and Don hadn't long retired from competition before the Australian Modern Pentathlon Association put forward the name of Judge John Xavier O'Driscoll for life membership. At the Australian association meeting, it seems the two newly elected members from the New South Wales association had other ideas. Not only did they refuse to rubber stamp the proposal, they rejected the judge's nomination outright. The negative votes were cast by the recently elected New South Wales representatives who happened to be the recently retired Donald McMiken and Duncan McIntyre Page. It had taken them a while but there would be no more scooping up loose change from the floor. They owed the man nothing, and nothing is exactly what he got.

Don was not the only one to experience difficulty with money that was promised. Before the Tokyo Olympics, in what was seen as a fine gesture, the St George Rugby League Club invited Duncan to a ceremony with a few other Olympians to accept a cash gift for expenses incurred along the way. It was good PR for a club that liked to recognise one of their own, even if Dunc's promising career had been nipped in the bud. Pagey duly presented himself to the small group that congregated at the entrance to the famous League's club, known locally as 'The Taj Mahal'. A previous Olympic swimmer, whose name Pagey can't recall, shook his hand and passed over an envelope. The local paper took pictures, and all was well in hand. The recipient was duly grateful, mouthed some appropriate words and then out the door he went. On his way to the car, Dunc opened the envelope to trouser the promised cash donation. He looked and then looked again. The envelope was empty. Hard to believe but considering the treatment the Pentathlon Three were accustomed to receiving, it wasn't all that much of a surprise.

22

STRANGE TIMES IN MEXICO

Duncan Page has never shown any real interest in politics – certainly not during the sixties, and even less in the present. Even so, he was a first-hand witness to the social revolution sweeping the world in the mid to late sixties of that tumultuous decade. It all seemed to come to a head at the 1968 Mexico Olympics – on the streets of the city as well as in the stadium. Before returning to the land of Zapata and Villa, Pagey was trying to chat up the Little Mermaid in Copenhagen. There is a lovely picture of 'Denmark Dunc' getting up close and personal with her. The lady was uncommunicative, but he put that down to her having a bad day. After his Copenhagen brush off, it was off to Jönköping in the south of Sweden for the World Modern Pentathlon Championships.

As expected, the pentathlon ride was a never-ending source of drama. Spectacular horsemanship and equally spectacular falls. The two went hand in hand, and no one was immune from the latter. The mount Dunc drew came with a bad reputation. It was the kind of horse that simply would not jump. 'When I found out, I knew this was going to be interesting.' He went on to elaborate: 'When a horse is about to refuse a jump, he digs his heels in. You can actually feel it.' What to do? Dunc pondered his dilemma as he rode down the laneway taking the competitors to the start of the ride. Peter Cayley, Australia's team manager and a noted equestrian rider, saw Dunc passing and quietly asked, 'I've got a pair of sharp spurs, do you want them?' The answer was an unequivocal 'yes' and the transfer occurred in a couple of seconds. As expected, when the horse came to the first jump it tried to refuse, but with a not so gentle prod of Peter Cayley's spurs, the hitherto reluctant mount 'just soared over the obstacle'. Dunc persuaded his now-reformed mount to complete the course with flawless ease. Pagey had a clear ride that saw him in the lead until the last couple of riders. Pagey's final result was a sharp third placing.

STRANGE TIMES IN MEXICO

After his ride, and 'before I could walk away', Dunc was approached by an official who informed him that the jury would like to examine his spurs. That could have proved dicey but as luck would have it, as soon as the ride was over, he and the team manager made a quick exchange and Pagey was back to his original spurs. Sharpened spurs safely in the pocket of his coat, Peter Cayley presented a picture of righteous innocence.

There was more individual success in the shoot where he came second by 'a point' to a Hungarian. Duncan made no mention of the number of pistols the Hungarian government provided its shooters, but if it was anything like the épées they had on offer, his opponent would have had an impressive arsenal at his disposal. Again, Pagey rated the team's overall performance as 'Just average. Nothing special'. After Sweden, it was back to Oz and the Melbourne trials where the team for Mexico would be selected. The trial results were exactly what they always were – Peter leading Dunc and Don in that order. Once more, Lloyd Mitchelson was made the reserve. That didn't go down well with the perpetually disgruntled Lloyd. It got even worse when Don had a poor ride, and Lloyd just managed to pip him. The violins came out, and the old 'I was twice Australian Pentathlon Champion' lament grated on eardrums. The selectors were deaf to his music because they stayed with the same team that finished so impressively in 1964. Official letters received; it was viva Mexico '68 for the Pentathlon Three.

While packing his bags Dunc left room for his cache of double bungers and a new delivery mechanism – a shanghai (also known as a 'slingshot' or 'catapult'). The secret stash would be useful, he thought, during idle moments in the Olympic Village. 'I made sure I had a plentiful supply with me. You had to have a laugh.' For hyper fit young men with time on their hands, the inevitable consequence is that boys are more than likely to be boys. Imagine anyone trying to smuggle that kind of contraband onto a plane in the current era. In very short order, Dunc would have found himself representing his country at Long Bay. But those were kinder times and the intention was entirely harmless. Not that the recipients of a double bunger attack found it as amusing as the perpetrators.

After finding their room in the Olympic Village and settling in, the boys had a good look around. From their lofty accommodation on the third floor of the athlete's quarters they surveyed the scene that unfolded below. It wasn't long before they spotted two female Russian athletes entering the women's compound. The opportunity was too good to miss. Out came the trusty shanghai. And didn't it work a treat. With impressive accuracy, the double bunger landed right behind the Russki ladies and detonated with an impressively loud explosion. In the aftermath of the sneak attack, a scene of frantic activity developed on the streets below. The women scurried for safety while police materialised from thin air. There were 'sirens, search lights and vehicles; the whole shooting match'. Mexican cops were 'running around everywhere'. 'It was night-time, so you can imagine the confusion and the noise. It was quite a spectacle.' Very carefully the boys moved away from the window and found something else to occupy their idle hands.

Another irresistible opportunity arrived the very next day. On this occasion Pagey and Don were visiting the New Zealand dorm on the second floor when a couple of Cuban athletes sauntered past under the window. It is worth pausing to recall that this was a time of great hostility between Cuba and the United States. Relations were extremely precarious. It is fair to say that the international ramifications were not a concern for the two Aussies as they lit a bunger and dropped it behind the Cubans. The bunger went off as programmed and the targets dived for safety. Pagey swears he heard one of them yell 'Ay caramba!' – but accepts that in the heat of the moment he may be mistaken. The Cubans picked themselves up and spotted the New Zealand flag proudly displayed from the open window. They made a beeline for the Kiwi room, but the real culprits hadn't waited around. They were long gone by the time the irate Cubans came looking for revenge. It was up to their Commonwealth cousins to explain themselves.

If that near miss wasn't enough, there was more to come. Seeking further opportunities from their third-floor aerie, they saw an open window across the road from which emanated the sound of merriment. They couldn't help themselves – the shanghai was reloaded and a bunger hurtled toward the open window. With what was, Pagey admits, 'a complete fluke', the projectile found its target with unerring accuracy and exploded with a resonance that was more than satisfactory. The shouting and swearing that ensued would have peeled the paint – there were 'fellows running everywhere'. All up it was a brilliant outcome for a modest investment at a hardware shop in a small Victorian country town. Pagey's final words on the matter provide their own explanation, 'When you were young, mate'.

Fun and games aside, they had come to Mexico to compete, and soon enough the day arrived. The skylarking had to end sometime and, unfortunately, it ended with an unexpected step backward for the Pentathlon Three. After their encouraging fifth in the previous Olympics, the team slid back to a disappointing eleventh in Mexico. One of the chief suspects, which affected all the competitors who lived and trained at sea level, was the altitude of Mexico City. There was no escaping it. Dunc is adamant that 'the altitude killed me in the run'. It had a similar effect on unparalleled athletes like the great Australian distance runner, Ron Clarke, who, after the ten thousand, collapsed with altitude sickness and had to be resuscitated by the team doctor. Pagey observes that Ron was beaten in the ten thousand by athletes who lived and trained at altitude. And he wasn't alone. 'No one could run there. Look at what happened to Clarkey. The funniest thing about trying to run at altitude is that you just can't breathe. You could walk around town and you didn't notice it but once you put in an effort, it really hit you. I wasn't long into the run before I was struggling to breathe, and it was no different in the swim.'

The ride was a source of considerable consternation. The host nation devised a challenging course that ended with a highly unusual obstacle – a house. That's right, a house. The riders were required to guide their mounts into the house, around a table, out the back door and then over its back fence which also served as the final jump. Dunc came a creditable fourth and remembers the final obstacle with great amusement. 'Only in Mexico, mate. It's a different world. A different world.' Wherever he rode, and not just in Mexico, the words of the exacting equestrian coach at Fort Sam remained front and centre. 'The Colonel did us a favour by making us get our riding legs "in" every day except Sunday. He insisted that we had to give our horses every possible chance to get over the obstacle. He warned us not to try anything funny. If you don't know the horse, it was up to you to present him to a jump in the best possible way. Most of all he taught us always to be prepared for the unexpected.' The lessons of Fort Sam remained with some of Colonel Russell's students but not so much for some others. The excellent results Dunc achieved in the ride are testament to his ability to listen and then implement the lessons he took away from Fort Sam.

He needed all of Colonel Russell's accumulated wisdom in the ride. Pete and Don each had a hard time in their rides so it fell to Dunc to complete the course as best he could. He describes it as 'a difficult ride because Peter and Don had poor rides and I had to ride safely and stay in control'. Never had the necessity to put John Russell's words into practice been so urgent. Dunc got around the course and when he crossed the line, Neville Sayers, the team manager, later wrote that Duncan had ridden 'magnificently'. Pagey isn't so sure about the magnificent bit and prefers to say that his ride was 'nothing special, just careful'. Not only is the man unstoppable in his sporting ambitions, he is equally relentless in his modesty when attaining them.

Dunc's observation that Mexico 'is a different world' became seriously apparent in the government's solution to problems that threatened to disrupt the games. All through North America at that time there was considerable social upheaval stemming from the civil rights movement and the Viet Nam war protests. Mexico was not immune, and its activists and students emulated their northern neighbours. Pagey recalls hearing machine gun and rifle fire as he lay in bed at night. There were reports that two thousand students had been shot. When things settled down, he was taken for a drive around town by an expat family friend. As they drove past the university, Dunc saw unmistakable evidence of civil unrest – 'They must have used artillery to shoot the entrance gates off their hinges, and you could see where the brick work was chipped with machine gun fire'. Another night, he was driven into the city for a look around and, when they tried to return, the 'fighting going on' was so severe that 'we had to take a hundred mile detour to get back to the village'. A member of the Mexican pentathlon team later took Dunc aside and quietly informed him that the government was disposing of the bodies in an industrial furnace not too far from the games site.

The unrest came to a head inside the stadium itself during the medal ceremony for the men's two-hundred metre race. The event was taken out in world record time by the American, Tommie Smith, with his compatriot, John Carlos, finishing third. The two Yanks were split by Peter Norman, one of Australia's finest ever male sprinters. Not only could Peter run, he was an outstanding human being. In the build-up to the medal ceremony Tommie Smith and John Carlos, both African Americans and strong supporters of the civil rights movement, were discussing a plan of action. They were made aware of the scandalous treatment of the Mexican protesters and were determined to come up with the best way of making a gesture to support their brothers in both countries. What happened next was a sensation seen throughout the world. Both men raised a black-gloved fist during the national anthem in an unmistakable 'Black Power' salute. Peter Norman, who was in on the plan, offered his unhesitating support saying, 'I will stand with you'. He asked what he could do. The Americans suggested he wear a badge for the Olympic Project for Human Rights. Peter didn't raise his fist, but the badge, also worn by the others, was the statement of a highly principled man. The photographs of the three sprinters on the podium says it all – and didn't it cause a stir. The two Americans were summarily thrown out of the Olympic Village and ostracised by the Olympic movement for years after. Peter Norman suffered a similar fate when he returned home. He was vilified and treated as a pariah by the press and the Olympic supremos. Worse was to come when he was overlooked for the 1972 Olympic team even though he was the current Australian two hundred metre record holder. The selectors solved that inconvenient problem by deciding not to send anyone to run the two hundred. It is a national disgrace that it took the Sydney Olympics coming to town in 2000 before the Olympic big shots relented and recognised his contribution. When Peter died in 2006, as a sign of deep respect for their Australian mate, the Americans with whom he shared the Mexican podium showed up to carry his coffin. To this day, John Carlos refers to Peter Norman as 'my brother'. In deep historical irony, half a century later the Australian two hundred metre record is still held by none other than Peter George Norman. To this day, no one has managed to better it. Sadly, the record wasn't good enough to earn him a spot at the '72 Olympics.

And who happened to be sitting in the stands during that momentous medal ceremony? Duncan McIntyre Page, of course. 'Mate, I was in the stands looking down. Don't ask me how I got there, but I was there.' Not only was he an observer of that historic event but, unlike the cheapskate treatment they received in Tokyo, this time the boys were allowed to march in this closing ceremony. And march they did – proudly and side-by-side with the rest of the Olympic team. On the way to the Stadium, Dunc couldn't help but notice that the streets leading up to the stadium entrance were lined with soldiers armed with rifles. In an unsuccessful attempt at concealment, the soldiers were crouched behind the bushes. The attempt at being unobtrusive was laughable. All the same, the world audience watching on TV saw only the fun and the laughter. 'The average punter wouldn't have known anything about what really went on.' The athletes and the people of Mexico City knew. And the ever-observant Duncan Page certainly knew, as did his fellow Olympians Peter Norman, John Carlos and Tommie Smith. But the American duo weren't present at the closing ceremony. By then they had been sent home in disgrace. Peter Norman would suffer his own special ignominy at the hands of officialdom and the press as soon as he stepped off the plane at Mascot.

Officialdom. A strange word for a strange breed. Words do not come easily when describing the actions of certain decision-makers within the Australian Olympic 'family'. Common terms like 'short-sighted', 'stupid', 'ignorant', 'boneheaded', 'intransigent', and so on, are inadequate because they cannot encompass the lasting effects of the breathtaking ineptitude displayed by the blazers. Take the pentathlon association's attitude to its own athletes. It was customary for other countries when hosting the world championships to allow their riders to acquaint themselves with the riding course before the other competitors arrived. Not only did that allow them intimate familiarity with the course, it gave them the opportunity to ride all the horses. Were the Pentathlon Three afforded the same privileges when Oz hosted the world championships? No chance. The poobahs demurred in a classic case of holier-than-thou fluff and floss. 'The highest standards of probity must be maintained. Give our lads an advantage over other countries? Wouldn't think of it. Must be seen to do the right thing.' That load of bollocks nearly brought Dunc undone at the Melbourne world championships when, before the ride, a Mexican pentathlete approached him to enquire about the horse he had drawn. Poor Dunc. With open-handed honesty, he confessed that he had no idea. 'We weren't allowed to go anywhere near them', he told the sceptical enquirer. With a knowing look the Mexican said, 'You, Señor Page are not telling me the truth.' (Spanish does not contain the soft 'g' sound – 'g' as in 'giant'. So, for him, it was 'g' as in 'goddammed liar'). To prove his bona fides, Pagey raced around until he located the owner of the Mexican's horse. He managed it somehow, and the info about the horse was duly passed on. Another international incident narrowly avoided.

Petty theft was another no-no. The blokes in blazers excelled themselves in the aftermath of the Tokyo games by expelling the great Dawn Fraser. Dawn's heinous crime? In a post-games bout of skylarking she pinched a flag, and for that she was cast into Australian Olympic purgatory. There was a great hullabaloo and an unsavoury aftermath. 'Our Dawn' was officially barred from the next games. The consequences were typical – another potential gold medal down the drain. Tossed out because in a light-hearted moment she pinched a bloody flag? Dawn was far from alone when it came to Olympic petty theft. Indeed, Pagey is himself an extremely lucky man. Had the blazers discovered his disgraceful escapade after Mexico, who knows what his fate may have been? Drummed out of the regiment? Buttons sliced off by a sabre at dawn? But then again, the blazers probably wouldn't have bothered. 'Duncan Page? Who's he? Oh, quite. A pentathlete, you say? Not sufficiently high profile. Would scarcely rate a mention and anyway we wouldn't get our names in the paper.'

Pagey's flaggary (a legal term denoting the theft of flags and banners) was easily the equal of Dawn's. It is fair to say that his misdemeanours were conducted with infinitely greater precision and forethought. Unlike Ms Fraser's one-off escapade, this was not the first time this particular culprit had committed the offense. It is apparent now that Duncan McIntyre Page was a serial offender when it came to flaggary. His rap sheet includes thefts in Switzerland and Mexico and most likely other places to which he is yet to own up. The Swiss heist first. The world pentathlon championships in that country had concluded. The only things left were flags emblazoned with the logo and the words, 'World Pentathlon Championships'. Pagey had a burning desire to obtain one of the banners by any means – fair or foul. Fair was obviously out of the question, so foul it had to be. The night was dark as he crept through the bushes and started cutting at the ropes supporting the flag. While so engaged, he heard rustling in the bushes behind him. His heart stopped, 'I thought I'd been sprung'. To Dunc's immense relief, the head that poked through the foliage belonged to David Kirkwood, his American mate from Fort Sam. Dave was intent on a similar mission. Dunc got what he wanted, and Dave helped himself to a couple of other flags. Then they hid the purloined items 'in the bush along the road'. The flag thefts did not go unnoticed. Not in orderly Switzerland they didn't. For days after, every bag, trunk or suitcase leaving each pentathlete's accommodation was thoroughly examined. Unsuccessfully, it seems. They had vanished without trace until . . . on the bus taking them away from the venue, Dave and Dunc asked the driver to stop so they could answer nature's call. They sauntered into the bush and returned with stolen goods in hand. This book marks the first public acknowledgement of a crime that sorely puzzled the Swiss authorities. If there is any justice in the world, Mr

STRANGE TIMES IN MEXICO

Page may now expect a letter of demand from the Swiss consulate. On certain occasions the stolen banner has surfaced, displayed to great effect across the verandah of a certain Bundeena waterfront house.

Another incident of attempted flaggary involving Mr Page occurred during the post-Olympic celebrations at a swanky golf club in Mexico City. The driveway leading up to the venue was festooned with flags of various nations and Pagey's eye was drawn to the Mexican flag which stood out from the others because it was bedecked with gold braid. The moment he saw it, the flag was as good as on the way to Oz. During the meal, and after pocketing a steak knife, he rose from the table and casually headed for the men's room. Once out of sight, he ducked out the front door and went straight to the flagpoles. By now an expert flaggarist, Dunc cut the ornate ensign loose, quickly wrapped it up and went over to the Australian team bus where he stashed it under his seat. At that critical moment, just as he was about to straighten up, he felt a pistol pressed firmly against his ribs. Pagey's immediate response? 'I hope your pistol doesn't have a hair trigger mate.' The security guard was not the kind to ask politely, 'Habla español?' Not with his gun jammed against the ribs of a thieving gringo. So Dunc was marched unceremoniously to the manager's office. Fortuitously, it was located at the side of the club so Dunc was spared the embarrassment of being paraded like a common criminal before his fellow Olympians. The manager eyed off the captive with an amused twinkle and proceeded to address him in a thick Scots brogue. He grinned and advised Dunc that he had made a bad mistake. 'Someone saw you laddie, and ye got caught.' The Scotsman, who 'took it as a bit of a joke', waved it off and allowed the relieved flaggar to rejoin the festivities.

Two minor matters remain. The first occurred with Dunc sitting on the bus just as they were leaving the golf club. After that close shave he was counting his blessings when another security guard, responsible for retrieving and stashing all the ceremonial flags at the back of the bus, asked the chastened Pagey, 'Señor will you watch these flags for me por favor? Some bad hombre ees trying to steal them.'

Then there is the lovely Maria Elena part two. Pagey had kept her phone number all those years and, with the help of a Games interpreter called the hacienda and asked to speak to the lovely señorita. The interpreter dialled the number, inquired, and listened for a long time. When she hung up, she gave Dunc a radiant smile and informed him that Maria Elena had married extremely well to a rich Yanqui and is happily living in Texas. Lucky her – she won the lottery. Every señorita's dream is to marry a rich American who will sweep her off her feet and take her away. As for Dunc's own dreams – he isn't saying. As for the ornate Mexican flag – 'In the end it stayed where it was'. And then, with the rhetorical flourish of a seasoned criminal, Pagey sighs, 'Ah well, such is life'.

23

HOUSE HUNTING

By the end of 1968, Dunc arrived back from Mexico in need of a reality check. It was finally time he faced the facts and Father Time. The inevitable stared back at him in the mirror. The reflection said that he had reached the end of an illustrious sporting career. Despite numerous setbacks that would have stopped lesser men cold, he had achieved all his primary goals. The evidence was right before his eyes. With every stroke of the razor, the inexorable toll of wear and tear on the human body became increasingly apparent. Time to find a different way of going. But what to do? The other two members of the Pentathlon Three had their houses in order. Peter went back to work for the police and then to another two Olympics. Don was pursuing his successful academic career in animal and human physiology. Pagey? Well, it was business as usual for a while. The saddlery which provided leather goods for the George Street gun shops continued apace. He still competed as a pentathlete but his interest gradually waned until it stopped altogether.

The time had come to take a good hard look at himself. Hadn't he accomplished what he set out to do? Had he not represented his country? Had he not played for the greatest rugby league club of all time? Had he not won an Australian Surf Lifesaving Club beach sprint championship? Had he not represented his country at the Olympics with distinction – and done so twice? There was precious little left to accomplish. When he looked at it that way, Dunc had to admit that there wasn't much more he could have done. Regrets? He had a few. What could he have accomplished if he hadn't been impeded by his bung leg? Crook appendage or not, he still helped the team to a respectable fifth in Tokyo. With two good legs would the boys have stood on the podium? Almost certainly. Before his injuries, Dunc had been an outstanding runner at distance as well as hurdles and sprints. A fully functional leg would also have improved his swim results. The proof of that? When Terry Gathercole had them swim without kicking, Dunc consistently beat the others home. But that was all conjecture. His accomplishments were a matter of record and now he could sit back and be justifiably proud of them. It was time to move on. There were many productive years ahead of him.

The reason for Dunc's retirement from competitive sport (temporary though it turned out to be) was in response to biological and emotional imperatives which had their origins in 1966. That was the year when Jim Kerr, an American pentathlete, visited him at his Blakehurst home. Pagey, who is hospitable to a fault, enjoyed showing Jim the sights of Sydney. On one occasion, while on their way to somewhere, they passed by an extremely appealing blonde lady walking along the footpath near the Page residence. The American visitor, who Dunc describes as a 'world class pants man', yelled out, 'Drive back around the block'. Pagey obliged, but the attractive blonde had disappeared. A disappointed Jim Kerr shrugged his shoulders and Dunc quickly forgot all about the vanishing blonde. And there it stayed – a matter of case closed, until . . . shortly after his return from Mexico, he drove down the same street. This time Pagey couldn't help but notice an attractive pair of legs protruding from beneath a vehicle. The legs belonged to a young woman working industriously on her car's undercarriage. 'Can I give you a hand there?' A logical question to ask a pair of beautiful legs. Hearing the question expressed so politely, the person attached to the legs emerged from beneath the car. Surprise, surprise. The legs belonged to the same blonde Jim Kerr spotted two years earlier. Indeed, it was the very same person, and her name was Carol. As they have a way of doing, things steadily progressed. In short order, Dunc learned that commitment to a relationship and commitment to his sport did not go hand in hand. The time had come to pull the pentathlon plug.

Absolute determination in the pursuit of a goal has always been the Page hallmark and it was on full display in the burgeoning relationship. He and Carol got serious and, after several trips down the South Coast, they found a spectacular block of land at Manyana where they built themselves a holiday home. Holiday home? How can you have a holiday home when you don't own a real home? Dunc was aware of the incongruity and immediately set off to find a house in Sydney. It made sense. Both he and Carol were working. The saddlery business was ticking over nicely. No more pentathlon expense and no need for temporary loans from Mick Simmons, thank you very much. For once the stars aligned in his favour – the time was right to find a house. It became even more right when, from out of the blue, the business deal of a lifetime landed in his lap.

There were definite similarities in the way Dunc went about finding a house and his approach to training for Modern Pentathlon. It was done methodically, single-mindedly and unsparingly. Pagey reminds anyone who cares to listen that whatever success he had was because 'I always worked harder than most'. His approach to finding that perfect block of land at Manyana is instructive. After several weekends poking around the South Coast, he and Carol came to a joint decision – that was the general area for them. Carol had long expressed a preference for a waterfront property and that became music to Dunc's ears. Her wish became his command, so he promptly set off on a self-appointed mission to find one. With commendable thoroughness, he wrote to every owner of every block of waterfront land at Manyana. The letter, phrased respectfully, boiled down to a simple question: 'Are you interested in selling?' Despite its polite tone, the letter received just one reply. And that was all it took. Luck's a fortune because the reply was from a bloke in need of ready cash. In due course, Dunc was the proud owner of a block on Manyana's headland sporting panoramic north to south coastal views. He then whacked up a kit home that bravely withstood the region's punishing southerlies. Dunc and Carol had a waterfront beach house, but they still had nowhere to live in Sydney.

With the precedent of Manyana behind him, Dunc used a similar modus operandi to find the right type of house in the right part of Sydney. Ought to be a piece of cake, he naively thought. Unfortunately, buying Sydney real estate is an infinitely different proposition from buying into the quiet and orderly South Coast market. With Carol's expressed desire to live on the water at the forefront of his thinking, Dunc's 'your wish is my command response' was as strong as ever. In an arc that stretched from Kyle Bay on the George's River to Sans Souci on Botany Bay, his objective was clear – find a house somewhere along that 5.2 kilometre stretch. There was much more ground to cover and shoe leather to expend in approaching each house. It was a thankless task; walking through front yards to knock on doors and trudging away defeated yet again. But persistence and determination are two of the Page family's cardinal virtues, so Dunc kept chipping away. Then one day he came upon a Kogarah Bay house with a 'For Sale' sign out front. Full of great expectations, Pagey knocked on the door. It was opened by the guardedly welcoming but no-nonsense owner. The bloke listened to what Dunc had to say, thought about it, and then said, 'Let's talk'.

And that's how Pagey met Fred Hollows. A younger generation may not be familiar with Fred's contributions to ophthalmology and his magnificent work throughout the world, especially among Australia's First Nations people, but his provision of health care to the disadvantaged was outstanding. The foundation that bears his name continues the legacy of achievement he worked tirelessly to establish. The public persona of Fred Hollows as a lovable eccentric was on full display during the subsequent real estate negotiations – as the eager young man standing on his doorstep will attest. Dunc's rueful recollection is that 'he would be as eccentric as anyone you would run into'. The negotiations were protracted and came attached with a tricky precondition. The vendor was happy to sell and the cashed-up purchaser was keen to buy; but . . . 'I've got one condition; you've got to find me a house at Hunter's Hill'. Pagey learned of that condition while Fred was in the company of two gentlemen on day release from Long Bay Gaol. Fred took great delight introducing his companions, one of whom he explained was a double murderer and the other was responsible for only one. Despite such minor distractions, negotiations proceeded on their delicate way. Curiously, the Hunter's Hill precondition, despite being 'such an outrageous demand', wasn't an immediate deal breaker. 'At the time I thought, "That's no problem, I'll be able to do that".' Upon

HOUSE HUNTING

reflection, Dunc had second thoughts. He asked Professor Hollows, 'What say you don't like the house I've found you?' A sensible enough question. The reply was equally sensible. 'Then you'll have to keep looking until you find me a house I like.'

It was obvious by then that things were going nowhere fast, but Pagey was nothing if not determined. Carol would have her house on the water, come what may. 'You want something, you've got to try to go out and get it.' For a while, he continued the search for Fred's house at Hunter's Hill, but also decided to have a look elsewhere. He was hedging his bets. And Dunc knew exactly where to start looking – in the Saturday edition of the *Herald* of course. In its glory days the Saturday edition of the *Sydney Morning Herald* with its endless pages of advertising – Kerry Packer famously described them as 'rivers of gold' – contained a mammoth real estate section. It was mandatory reading for Sydney real estate addicts – and their numbers were legion. Tucked among the fine print was an advertisement for a waterfront property in the tiny community of Bundeena just across the Hacking River from Cronulla. Enveloped by the majestic bush of Royal National Park, at the time Bundeena was a natural jewel that glistened in Sydney's crown. He and Carol had a look. The house needed a bomb under it, but the block was sublime. 'This is better than Fred's', was their joint opinion, and all further negotiations ended then and there. From then on, the great Fred Hollows would have to peruse the real estate section in the *Herald* all by himself.

The Bundeena transaction came with its own inherent difficulties. The house had been left to three elderly ladies who couldn't decide what to do with it. The options ranged from living in it to selling up and moving on. Fortunately for Dunc, the latter prevailed. A reasonable offer was made and accepted. That was all well and good until the solicitor decided to take his own sweet time about attending to the legals. The ladies were getting edgy and the deal looked like it was going west. 'You couldn't blame them. They wanted their brass mate.' The matter came to a head when a determined Duncan Page stormed into the office of the indolent suburban solicitor. He informed the receptionist that he needed the documents signed, and he needed them immediately. The receptionist tartly informed him, 'Oh no sir, it could take another couple of weeks at least'. Dunc knew that the old girls weren't going to wear that and, in his present mood, neither would he. On came the competition face with its look of absolute concentration. 'Right then, I'll just wait here until you hand over the documents.' The alarmed receptionist, seeing the grim look of the man, disappeared into her boss's office. She reappeared in 'about five minutes' and wordlessly handed over the documentation. Paperwork in hand, the deal was sealed and Pagey and Carol got to work pulling down the old place and putting up a new one.

House-hunting and house-buying are completely different disciplines. With patience and time, it's not difficult to find the house. Signing on the dotted line? That's another thing altogether. First and foremost, the buyer has to have the readies or at least a helpful bank prepared to provide them. Luckily for Dunc, at the time he was looking and buying he was also rolling in cash. The cold hard fact is that when he got back from Mexico, he walked off the plane stony motherless broke – yet again. And yet somehow, in a few short months, there he was, cementing a lifelong relationship and demonstrating his bon fides by coming up with the cash for the Bundeena property. So where does a penniless pentathlete find that kind of money? He earns it of course – with a dollop of blind luck and a dash of good management.

Whatever he was, Duncan Page was never afraid of hard work. After Mexico he got straight into it in the shed in Cy and Jessie's backyard. Soon he was churning through the leather and keeping the George Street gun shops well stocked with holsters and cartridge belts. It was a reliable earner but not enough to keep the banks happy when he came knocking. Not if he had to go cap in hand to buy a house. When he got around to relating the story of how he found the cash, Pagey is the first to admit that 'an ounce of luck is worth a tonne of judgement'. The ounce of luck arrived unannounced one day while Dunc was hard at work in the Blakehurst backyard. A bloke showed up and wanted to talk, so Pagey downed tools and listened. Today he is embarrassed to confess that he didn't have the presence of mind to invite the man inside and offer him a cup of tea. Instead they conducted their conversation on the front lawn. The man showed Dunc a diagram for a pouch he wanted made and asked if he thought could make him up a sample. The experienced saddler took a quick look at the specifications and said, 'No problem'. 'How much?' was the next question. 'Two dollars', came the reply. Dunc had the item, a pouch designed to carry a sheep drench dispenser, ready in a couple of days. It was duly picked up and the satisfied customer returned a couple of days later. 'Can you make me five more?' No problem again – they were made for the same price then picked up and paid for. A couple of days later, the man reappeared, this time to ask the question of a lifetime: 'Can you make me thirteen thousand of the pouches?' It was a backyard saddler's dream. Pagey took a deep breath, thought for two seconds and said, 'No problem'. After a major reorganisation of his work environment, he produced the pouches in 'a couple of months'. The sheep dip bloke was happy, Pagey was smiling and the money 'came rolling in'. It kept rolling when another order for eleven thousand pouches arrived on his work bench.

Even after the expense of setting up a factory and hiring staff, there was plenty of room for profit. Pagey's once in a lifetime sheep drench bonanza paid off big time. It meant that he was now able to come up with the cash for the Bundeena waterfront property. Carol would be living her waterfront dream while Dunc could set up his saddlery in a room with a view.

While Pagey was deeply involved with solidifying his financial and personal matters, the world of Modern Pentathlon continued on its merry way. Peter represented his country at two more Olympics, while Don was appointed manager of the Aussie team at the Montreal Olympics in 1976. In Montreal, Don had the dubious privilege of witnessing one of the most deplorable moments in the long history of the Olympics. The scandalous incident involved the Soviets – of course it did – but for once the drama had nothing to do with skulduggery or illegal chemical stimulants. Unusually for Modern Pentathlon, the drama didn't occur out on the equestrian course but during the fencing competition. Don was acting in his capacity as team manager when a kerfuffle broke out in a match between Jim Fox and the Soviet's Boris Onishchenko. Boris was a three-time world pentathlon champion and a particularly strong fencer. When he fenced the British team, the scoreboard registered a hit even though his opponent complained that Boris hadn't touched him. The complaint was initially dismissed. But it all came to a head when same thing occurred when Onishchenko fenced Jim Fox. Jim insisted that there had been no touch despite the scoreboard's recording one. The Brit, who afterwards maintained that he still considered Boris to be a mate, grabbed the Soviet's épée and demanded the officials examine it. To make a long story short, and despite Onishchenko's protestations that he didn't know whose épée it really was, the offending weapon was found to contain a sophisticated device that registered a hit when none had occurred. Fancy that, cheating at the Olympics. A Soviet athlete caught red-handed – who would have thought? And didn't that episode cause a stink. Don recalls seeing two burly Russians in plain clothes escorting Boris away. Onishchenko was immediately disqualified, and with that, the Commos had lost any chance for a medal. In a deliciously ironic twist, the Poms wound up taking out the gold medal.

24

A FOOL AND HIS MONEY

The day was no different from any other when he worked the horse along the beach at Boat Harbour near Kurnell. He walked the animal off the float and saddled it up. It was standard procedure before allowing it to stretch its legs over the packed sand by the shoreline. That day there was a minor difference to his usual routine – the saddle. The saddle he was using was borrowed leather. His own needed repair. He mounted the thoroughbred named 'Tensile' and trotted off before working it into a gentle canter. The rider's feet were secure in the stirrup irons as he idly recalled Colonel Russell's warning – 'Always be prepared for the unexpected'. Never had the dictum proved more apt and, as usual, the crusty old army officer was proved right. For some reason and, without warning, the borrowed saddle's stirrup leather broke on the offside. The rider was left with one foot wedged securely and the other dangling in the breeze. It was at this very moment that Tensile bolted. The sudden change of gait shifted the saddle under the horse. The rider was left with a predicament because he still had one foot securely lodged in the stirrup iron. Worse still, he now had a close up view of hooves flying past his head while he was dragged over the sand. A casual onlooker would have enjoyed the action of a good old-fashioned Western movie, especially when the other stirrup leather broke and the rider was left prostrate on the sand. The horse? Well, the riderless Tensile was last seen galloping toward the Tasman Sea.

The unhorsed rider was Duncan Page, of course. He lay wondering what hit him and assessed the extent of his injuries, all the while counting his lucky stars. 'That could have been the end of Dunc, mate.' Pagey picked himself up and, with the help of one of the workers at the nearby Kurnell sand mines, retrieved the spent Tensile. That single episode where he flirted with disaster is an appropriate metaphor for Dunc's long association with the racing 'game'. After much exposure to the training and racing of horses, he knew all about

Murphy's Law – 'Whatever can go wrong will go wrong'. The misadventure with Tensile also reflects his meticulous approach to conditioning thoroughbreds. Pagey applied his extensive experience of human physical conditioning to the equine world. He gave his horses lots of work, a practice that was then uncommon among Australian thoroughbred trainers. Dunc carefully recorded each horse's training schedule, which varied from dressage in the arena, to cross country, to interval work and, as at Kurnell, to days out at the beach. The intention was to get the horse superbly fit thereby giving it the best possible opportunity to win a race.

Not all trainers saw things Dunc's way, and the majority scorned his approach. Despite the sceptics, he persisted and was aided by two superb riders – Vicky Robinson and Robyn Thompson. These highly competent individuals followed Dunc's training schedules to the letter and helped him turn out some extremely fit racehorses. After that the future was in the lap of the gods. Unfortunately, the excellent conditioning program was wasted when the horses were placed in the 'care' of unsympathetic trainers. Dunc once brought a horse to a prominent city trainer who shall remain nameless. Pagey and his assistants presented him with a horse in peak condition and handed over the training schedules. The carefully prepared notes contained a detailed account of the work the horse had done over the past few months. It all came to naught when the trainer gave Dunc's notebook a cursory look before disdainfully throwing it on a nearby bale of straw. 'I don't need to look at that', was the dismissive response. Dunc's jaw dropped. He looked at the trainer in amazement but somehow maintained decorum. He still fumes about the trainer's off-handed response to this very day and has been heard to say, 'The ignorance of the man'. Conventional training orthodoxy of the day wasn't having a bar of this newfangled scientific approach. The old school maintained that things were just fine the way they had always been. 'Anyway, who's got the time to do all that extra work with the horses? We're flat out just doing what we're doing.' To a casual observer, what the old school said it was doing didn't amount to much when it came to their conditioning of racehorses.

A FOOL AND HIS MONEY

At the same time he was making his forays into the real estate market, Duncan was increasingly consumed by his racing interests. Over the coming years, these interests would cost him dearly in terms of time, money and, ultimately, grief. The love of horses was born into the boy and reached its full flower in the man. Pagey is the first to admit that he was 'always interested in horses'. It started with hacking Tommy and Ruby around the Blakehurst paddocks, and eventually led him to racetracks all around New South Wales. The man who could recite swathes of *The Man from Snowy River* was hopelessly addicted to the species equus. In plain English, Pagey couldn't keep away from the hayburners. Anyone who has stabled and fed a horse, most especially a non-performing racehorse, knows that it is an extravagantly expensive proposition. The drain on resources is both financial and emotional. Dunc sees that clearly from where he stands today, but back in the day it was a classic case of 'a fool and his money are soon parted'. Not that Dunc was ever a fool, but the dream of one day breeding a Melbourne Cup winner has been known to overpower even the most level-headed of men.

The truth is that Dunc's 'interest' in horses was more a lifelong love affair. Even so, the garrulous Terry Nichol once told anyone who cared to listen that he had 'taught Duncan to ride'. There seemed to be no limit to the fantasies of Freddy the Fibber. But Pagey's pentathlon rides were now ancient history and his present focus was on thoroughbreds. His interest was given added impetus when he was introduced to Bridget Woodford-Smith. Bridget was an impressive woman who owned and bred thoroughbreds. Shortly after they met, Bridget said that she had a horse stabled at Randwick and it was a bit of a handful. She asked Dunc if he would mind seeing what he could do with it. He was happy to oblige and, in his own words, 'I just hacked it about a bit'. Before long, the stroppy horse had learned to behave itself. Their initially casual relationship developed into a business relationship when they jointly purchased a brood mare. With that joint venture, the long journey from Oscar Myers's Blakehurst property to Randwick had come full circle.

Oscar was himself a multiple Royal Easter Show winner with little Tommy pulling a 'jogger' (a small sulky) and displaying his best manners. Following in his boss's footsteps, Duncan was soon competing on Big Red in horse shows at various locations – some nearby like the land that is today the Sutherland Hospital, to Mortdale and as far away as Kyeemagh near Mascot. At those events, the young rider was asked to demonstrate control of his mount. That was done, Dunc says, while 'I was sitting up on Red like a prize ponce'. These early competitions were an important milestone along the way to his subsequent achievements.

Another invaluable lesson came when the mature Pagey made the acquaintance of John Walsh, a Sydney medico who owned a string of polo ponies. The two men gravitated toward each other and often rode in each other's company. Hacking about with the good doctor's polo ponies was, Dunc says, crucial to developing his riding skills. John Walsh's property was heavily treed, and the ponies knew it well. Because of their familiarity, they constantly changed direction without warning. 'You had to be on your game, or you'd get wiped out on a tree.' The polo pony experience 'helped immensely' when it came to riding unfamiliar horses as was the norm in pentathlon events.

As well as dabbling in the real estate market, Pagey also obtained the owner/trainer's licence he needed to train and race thoroughbreds. Bridget Woodford-Smith and John Walsh provided glowing references; the kind preferred by the lofty Australian Jockey Club. In the fullness of time the AJC forwarded the licence, and at that precise moment Dunc's fate was sealed. His thoroughbred addiction reached full flower when he and Bridget went halves in a brood mare called 'Highland Sal'. They bought her at the fabled William Inglis Easter Sales. A problem slowly manifested itself with this particular arrangement. Initially Bridget and Dunc agreed that each partner would receive a foal in successive years. First year – Bridget got a foal. Second year – Highland Sal didn't get in foal. Next year – Bridget got another foal. The year after that – the mare didn't get in foal again. The on and off fertility cycle continued until an embarrassed Bridget handed the mare over saying, 'I've had my fair share of foals, Dunc, you can have her'.

A FOOL AND HIS MONEY

Now that he was sole owner of Highland Sal, Pagey enjoyed moderate success with a couple of her progeny. Not Melbourne Cup success, but two of Sal's foals developed into handy gallopers. Dunc took the youngsters under his wing and applied his training theories with the expert assistance of Vicky Robinson and Robyn Thompson. The first foal, a filly he called 'Bundeena Lass', won four races on country tracks. The second, a gelding called 'Highland Kid', was an impressive galloper who won five races, mostly on provincial tracks. Not a city winner between them but that was no disgrace. Winning at a city meeting is considered the hallmark of a good horse. Pagey owned and raced many horses but Highland Kid and Bundeena Lass were the best of the bunch.

Dunc had limited success with several other horses but that isn't a particularly impressive return for an adult lifetime devoted to breeding and training. Not impressive until you consider the facts of thoroughbred life. Of all horses bred and raced in Australia, only one in a hundred will go on to win a city race. One in fifty will win on a provincial track and one in twenty-five will win in the country. On these numbers, owning and racing a thoroughbred is a daunting proposition. But not for Pagey. The 'right' horse was always just around the corner. And, unstoppable as ever, Duncan Page was up for the challenge – the only obstacle was the size of his wallet. The limitations of his finances took Dunc along some interesting pathways and up a few blind alleys. Unable to bankroll his passion on his Pat Malone, Pagey had no option but to seek help from others. The people he found were not always well versed in the pitfalls of racing and their lack of knowledge was often embarrassingly on full display.

There was a chap, he shall remain nameless, who lived near Pagey. To the uninitiated at least, the bloke had all the swagger and appurtenances of the financially well off. This individual, we shall refer to him as Mr X, often expressed an interest in owning a racehorse. The interest grew until one day he asked Dunc to find him a suitable horse. Pagey did his due diligence and then it was off to the William Inglis and Son sales at Randwick. Back in the day, an Inglis horse sale was a big event. All the major players attended. Owners, trainers and jockeys congregated beneath the massive fig tree to rub elbows and converse in the arcane language of the racetrack. At this particular sale, the pre-eminent Sydney trainer of the era, TJ Smith, held court with champagne flute in hand. Lesser mortals looked on with a mixture of awe and envy. Most of them had to make do with a can of Tooheys. Pagey and his companion stayed away from the grog and concentrated on a fine little colt they hoped to pick up for a good price. While assessing its potential, Dunc patiently pointed out the horse's finer features. He spoke about its breeding and excellent physical attributes – solid reasons why it would attract a horseman's eye and potentially be a good purchase. Mr X then displayed his knowledge of horses by complimenting the owner for obviously having taken good care of the horse. He pointed to the straw bedding in the colt's box and said, 'Glad you have a lot for him to eat'. The owner didn't know which way to look and was even more taken aback when Mr X went on to ask in all seriousness, 'Will that horse grow a white star on its forehead?' The unspoken answer was, 'Not as long as your fundamental orifice points south mate'. But after a cautious look at Pagey, the owner ventured a speculative, 'You never know, maybe a star will appear one of these days'.

The faux pas continued when Peter Stuart entered the picture. Peter, himself a skilled equestrian, was Bridget Woodford-Smith's partner and a friend of Dunc's. Peter agreed to break in the horse at their property near Bowral. Mr X couldn't understand the need to ship the horse that far and solemnly assured everyone within earshot, there was 'lots of grass in my backyard'. Again no one said a word, although significant looks were exchanged. Assurances of the quantity and quality of the feed in his Bundeena backyard were followed up with another question. Mr X wanted to know if he could have a ride on the colt. Peter Stuart maintained a straight face and asked Mr X whether he had any riding experience. The reply came with the aplomb of a veteran of years on horseback, 'Sure I can ride, I spent a couple of days at Teen Ranch when

A FOOL AND HIS MONEY

I was younger'. Nothing was said, although what wasn't said would have filled volumes. As Pagey later observed, more in wonderment than unkindness, 'I never met anyone so naïve when it came to horses'.

Mr X was more than a wannabe racehorse owner. He was also something of a Lothario. In the company of his lady of the moment, he had often seen Dunc riding his surf ski at Bundeena. It looked easy enough, so he decided that he wanted a ski too and asked Pagey to find him something suitable. Dunc duly obliged but not before mentioning the caveat that, unless you have considerable experience with the craft, a surf ski can be a 'tippy' proposition. Mr X fancied that he could manage one without much difficulty, so he forked over the cash and took delivery of a nifty little blue number. The great reveal came on the day he entertained the latest of his love interests. Mr X picked up the ski and casually strolled down to where a choppy little shore break washed up. The instant he attempted to sit on his new ski, it shot off in all directions – none of them with its rider aboard. What should have been a lovely scene – handsome young man impressing awestruck maiden with his surf ski skills – well, it didn't happen. Dunc watched the display while seated beside the increasingly unimpressed damsel. History notes that the handsome young man then stalked up the beach, venting his spleen with each step. 'That surf ski you ordered for me is hopeless. It's lopsided and unbalanced. No one can ride it.' The tirade continued until Dunc said he would have a go with it. Your average human being, after copping such a spray, would have told the irate person just where he could stick his surf ski. But that is never Pagey's way. Ever the gentleman, he took a look at the ski. Not lopsided, not unbalanced. Hmm. So he hopped on the board and took it for a spin, expertly skidding above the choppy surf. Not a problem. It handled all right. Not as good as his board, but it would do in a pinch. Back on shore he handed it over to a speechless Mr X. The lovely maiden who witnessed all that? Her response is unrecorded as is the possibility that Dunc might have given her a knowing wink before he left.

As for the colt at the Inglis sale, which is where this tale started, Mr X, after displaying his ignorance of thoroughbreds, duly purchased the little colt and named it after the street on which he lived. Pagey remembers it as a 'very affable colt with no vices' and it went on to win a couple of country races. When the time came to retire the colt, Peter Stewart happily took it on as a hack at his Bowral property. With a bit of training, Peter said it turned out to be 'the best little cattle pony' he ever had and, together, they went on to win a few camp draft events.

That was not the last of Dunc's experiences with racehorse owners. In a moment of madness, the author agreed to take part in a syndicate that raced a fine-looking colt Pagey had bred. The other members of the syndicate, all with a cumulative knowledge of zero about racehorses, forked out their hard-earned money to train and race the horse. What an exercise in folly. Despites the owner's high hopes and its excellent breeding, the coal-black colt had difficulty running out of sight on a dark night. The trainer who agreed to take on the horse maintained a more balanced view of its prospects than its excitable owners. At one particular race meeting, he saddled the horse and quietly gave the jockey his riding instructions. A syndicate member approached respectfully to ask the trainer what he thought of the horse's chances. The trainer was not the kind to mince words. He gave his questioner a level look and said, 'Well, mate, I just told the jockey to bring a torch'. Translated from trainer's parlance, he was telling the hopeful questioner to keep his hands in his pockets. Why? Because the horse will still be running at sundown and the jockey will need a light to find the finish line.

An ounce of luck was often the missing element in Dunc's thoroughbred era. He had some wins and some losses, but says he was always hampered by 'circumstances'. The worst was the constant drain on his resources. Pagey couldn't afford to train the horses himself because of dire necessity – he had to beaver away at his saddlery business to have any hope of financing his dreams. That, in turn, left him at the mercy of trainers who either didn't understand or couldn't be bothered to find out how he had prepared his horses. Not only that, the fees top trainers charged were well beyond Dunc's limited budget. In consequence, he was forced to rely on the lesser lights. While the intentions of the people he employed may have been sincere, the quality of their work was often not up to scratch.

Dunc's fine horse, Highland Kid, is a case in point. To this day he says with deep regret, 'That horse could have been anything'. The Kid won a series of races in fine style and was scheduled to be given a run in a special three-year-old race at the Tamworth Gold Cup meeting. The horse's trainer and her partner floated the horse up to Tamworth and stabled him at the racetrack. For the first time, the Kid had the chance to test his mettle in a top field. Sadly for horse and owner, once again Lady Luck went missing in action. Along the way, as horses have a habit of doing, Highland Kid loosened a plate. The trainer's partner, either unwilling to wait for a farrier or trying to save money, took the job upon himself. With bated breath and much consternation, a small group of witnesses watched the man's amateurish efforts to reshoe the horse. In the end, he managed to 'prick' Highland Kid – he missed his hoof and drove the nail into the soft inner flesh. The upshot of that training disaster meant that a fine horse never got his chance. He was lamed by the kind of incompetence that comes with 'circumstances'. Worse was to come. The lamed horse developed an infection and was given penicillin. As luck would have it, the Kid was allergic to the drug and his head swelled to twice its normal size. When he finally recovered, most of his early dash was gone, and he never again performed up to his true potential. Veterans of the racing game would nod sagaciously and say to Pagey, 'Mate, if it wasn't for bad luck, you'd have no luck at all'.

There were rare moments of good fortune that arrived unexpectedly. Take the case of Rio Knights, a thoroughbred that came under Dunc's tutelage. Pagey had the horse in tip-top condition when he left him in the care of a thoroughbred trainer and prominent trotting driver. He happily pocketed the money and trained Rio Knights for a couple of outings only to watch the horse finish last or thereabouts. So undistinguished were the horse's efforts that, when the jockey dismounted, he told Dunc that Rio was 'the slowest horse

I've ever ridden. That thing is absolutely no good.' Howard Wilson concurred with the jockey's brutal assessment and demanded that Pagey remove the horse from his stables forthwith. Dunc demurred saying that the horse was entered for a race the following weekend at Nowra and they might as well let him have another go. The truculent trainer grudgingly gave the okay but insisted that Rio Knights must be out of his line of vision after that final race.

Dunc was happy with that arrangement and the next Saturday, it was off to Nowra for Rio Knights' swansong. When he got to the track, Dunc took up a position next to the trainer and his brother-in-law – another trainer whose horse was favourite in the race. The first thing Wilson said when Pagey arrived was, 'Did you bring your float? I'm not taking that horse back with me.' The brother-in-law then asked him, 'Is your horse any danger?' The reply was scathing, 'That horse is bloody useless. He's got no chance at all.' Dunc left the men to their deliberations and, as he was giving the jockey a leg up, he was asked the usual question – 'How do you want him ridden?' Pagey's quick answer was, 'Take him straight to the front and keep him there'.

And that is just what the jockey did. After the jump Rio was six lengths in front and stayed there for the entire distance, finishing first with a leg in the air. The trainer's brother-in-law looked at him in disgust. 'You told me your horse was no good and couldn't win.' The winning trainer ignored the complaint and told Pagey, 'We've found the secret'. After Rio Knights' stunning victory, there was no question of removing the horse from the stables and Dunc returned with an empty horse float. Rio Knights went on to win a couple more races and had a few creditable second placings before a fetlock injury forced him into retirement.

25

HARD BOILED

There was an American wrestler who plied his trade under the pseudonym of 'Hard Boiled Haggarty'. Unbeknownst to him, that particular grappler's name had a significant impact on later events far south of the equator. Pagey recalls one outing at the Sydney Pistol Club where two large professional wrestlers, with the names of Killer Karl Kowalski and Count Waldo Von Erich, happily blasted away at nearby targets. He found it interesting that his fellow shooters, despite their Eurocentric names, spoke to each other with strong Canadian accents. 'Good grouping, eh?' This brief encounter with the wrestling fraternity takes us directly to the other strong passion in Dunc's life – firearms and target shooting. The boy who nearly froze on top of a Vancouver mountain in pursuit of a firearm carried that passion throughout his adult life. The word 'carry' is used deliberately. It is a little-known fact that Dunc habitually carried one weapon or another on his person – most commonly a small Beretta .22 calibre pistol. Not that he ever used it. But wandering around the world armed with a pistol was a custom he brought home from the States. It was a habit that led to some interesting situations.

But back to the wrestling. Dunc and I made the drive to Tamworth to see Highland Kid run in the race that involved the gelding's disastrous encounter with incompetence. I was informed that we were to stay at a friend's house in the tiny town of Curlewis. The small town was pretty much a flyblown place but Mrs Haggart, mother of Fiona (Dunc's next-door Bundeena neighbour) and Annette, happily lived there with her husband in a lovely house. We never laid eyes on the husband, but Mrs Haggart was an engaging and generous hostess, as was Annette who politely put up with two strange men for a few days. Mrs Haggart was a lovely lady, and for reasons that are still unknown to her guests she was immediately given the nickname 'Hard Boiled Haggarty'. It was a misnomer of the highest order, but it stuck – especially when her visitors noticed several gaping holes in the backdoor fly screen. When asked about them, Mrs Haggart casually replied, 'Oh boys, that's where I shoot the snakes when they come slitherin' up the back steps'. We later located a 410 shotgun on top of a wardrobe and put two and two together. After her laconic country lady explanation, the 'Hard Boiled' nickname was a lock.

Curlewis is a good hour's drive from Tamworth, and each day we stayed there, Mrs Haggart started us off with a massive breakfast. Upon return we were met with an equally generous dinner. The intake of good country food forced Pagey to invest in several pairs of larger trousers when he got back to Sydney. After witnessing Highland Kid's botched re-plating, the drive back to Curlewis was somewhat subdued. It would have been funereal had we known the horse's adverse reaction to penicillin would terminate a singularly promising career. But we were younger men then and the following morning we were off to the races. After a dinner that had us groaning from oversupply, it was off to bed to prepare for the Tamworth Gold Cup.

Prior to arriving at the racetrack, Pagey stopped off at Tamworth's Commonwealth Bank to pay some bills. As soon as we entered the venerable building Dunc tossed me the small leather bag he habitually carried saying, 'I won't be long so, here, look after this'. I neatly caught the bag and retreated to a row of chairs lined against the wall. Waiting in a largish public building is never one of life's major pleasures and one quickly tires of people watching. Pension day in a bank soon degenerated into a playground for senior citizens. Pagey's bag offered a welcome diversion from the clientele. Upon closer inspection the bag created a sensation ranging between numb shock and deep horror. There, protruding from a small hole in the leather of the bag's bottom, was the unmistakable sight of the grey-black muzzle of a pistol. No matter how often I pushed it back into the bag, the muzzle cheekily reappeared. Hiding it on my person was out of the question and the consequences of being apprehended with a concealed firearm – in a bank no less – rapidly dawned on me. Stuffing the bag inside one's shirt was too obvious. Ditto for stuffing it down the front of one's trousers. A snoopy clear-sighted geriatric was bound to spring me.

A demand, all the more urgent for its silence, emanated across the crowded room. 'For crying out loud, Pagey, will you bloody well hurry up.' Seconds ticked over with languid regularity and took an eternity. At last, after what seemed hours later, Dunc concluded his business. The bag was restored to its rightful owner along with a searing admonishment about the consequences of carrying a concealed weapon. 'In a bank you silly bastard.' Pagey gave his admonisher a devil-may-care grin – the kind of smile given in similar circumstance by the likes of Butch to Sundance, by Frank to Jesse James and in all likelihood, given its Tamworth location, by Captain Thunderbolt to Frank 'The Darkie' Gardiner.

Pagey's close shaves and near misses didn't end at the bank in Tamworth. Nor did the carrying of concealed firearms. On another occasion Dunc sauntered through the airport on his way to a powerlifting competition (more about that later) this time with a similar bag and the same Beretta. He had been dropped off early and consequently had to hang around the departure lounge for 'hours'. Toward the end of his wait he watched a group of security men wrestle a portable metal detector into place. This was pre-9/11 and Australian airport security was at best ad hoc. Pagey wasn't concerned. He knew he was sweet because he had cleared security with bag and Beretta a couple of hours earlier. Not a problem. He landed in Canberra as casual as you please. A couple of days later on the return flight he had even better luck. It is accepted fact that civilised people don't wander about with concealed firearms on their person. You just don't do it. But Pagey did – and he did it with a blithe indifference to the consequences. Upon arriving in Sydney, he strolled down the arrival corridor with bag in hand until he came to another portable scanner. Had fate decreed that this was the moment he would finally be apprehended? Was he going to be caught red-handed? Not a chance. Not that day, not ever. One of the security blokes beckoned him through while the other said, 'Here, give me your bag'. No bells. No whistles. No strident alarm. Dunc passed through undetected and politely thanked the bloke who handed back his bag. That just doesn't happen in the real world, but it did for Pagey and his little Beretta.

Then there is the matter of the lost firearm. Dunc had ordered some leather for his saddlery and made the trip to Mascot to pick it up. The supplier provided him with an armful of tanned hides and when he got back to his car, Pagey discovered he was parked in front and back. With much sweat and fine manoeuvring he freed himself and returned to the safety of his workshop. As he unloaded the leather, he noticed that his bag – the one containing his wallet and firearm – was missing. Everyone is familiar with that instant of panic followed by the self-admonishment to 'settle down and think this through'. Where could it be? It wasn't in the back of the van. Must have fallen out where he had been parked in. There was a long drive back to Mascot but, 'Nope, not there either'. More thinking and then it was time to confess. Pagey rang the police from a nearby telephone booth. The duty officer, speaking in the professionally bored tones of officers when fielding calls about lost or stolen property, instantly was on the alert when he heard 'I have to report a lost firearm'. The cop read the riot act and Dunc learned he may be charged for a number of offences – most notably the failure to keep a firearm secure. Well, didn't that get the wind up the owner of the lost item. He raced back home and as he charged through the front door the phone was ringing.

Pagey manfully controlled his breathing as the person on the line asked, 'Is that Duncan Page?' 'That's me' was the guarded answer. 'Well I've found your bag and it has a pistol inside it.' Great sigh of relief. 'Was there any money in the bag?' In fact, there had been a lot of money in his wallet which had been in the bag, somewhere in the vicinity of four to six hundred dollars – a sizeable sum in those days. 'No mate, there was no money. Well at least I didn't see any. But I reckon the pistol must be worth a fair bit.' Pagey's reply was off-hand and dismissive. 'No mate, it's just a knockabout pistol and not worth a crumpet.' A disappointed silence on the other end. After a bit of to-ing and fro-ing Dunc arranged to drive to the factory where the man worked and reclaim the well-travelled Beretta.

Pistol retrieved, there remained the matter of pending police charges. What to do? The answer was bleedingly obvious. Did he not have a long-standing contact among the senior levels of the New South Wales Police force? Of course he did, so a phone call was hastily made. The person on the other end of the line listened attentively, cleared his throat and uttered his opinion. 'Well mate, the first thing you did wrong was you told the truth. You need to make up a story and stick to it no matter what. That's what all the crims do – not saying you're one of them of course.' Dunc thanked the senior officer for his professional advice and said his goodbyes. He thought carefully and then acted on advice. In short order, he concocted a story that sounded entirely plausible – at least to him.

The officer was less than thrilled as he listened to the newly minted explanation of how the Beretta had been lost and found. Plausible? You be the judge. 'Well officer, when I thought I had lost the pistol I contacted you straight away. Then I had another thought that I might have left it under some leather in the back of my van and guess what? It had been there all along. Sorry to trouble you but it is now safely back in my possession.' As professionally advised, Dunc had his story down pat and he stuck to it; all the while ignoring the obvious disappointment emanating from the other end of the phone. It seems that even back in those days the police were never happy unless they were fining someone for some offence or another – all in their role of de facto revenue collectors for state governments. In law enforcement, the more things change the more they stay the same.

All this was happening while, unknown to him, Dunc's financial affairs were heading for a major economic downturn. A recession in the Page economy was inevitable, especially after he experienced two successive shocks. The first involved an interesting discussion with a police procurement officer; the second was Martin Bryant's insane rampage through Port Arthur. The portents were grim. Taking the police matter first – Pagey innocently applied for a contract to make equipment for the force – something he was entirely qualified to do. After all, he had made equipment for the cops for many years. Innocently assuming the procurement procedure was legit, he bought a leather goods factory at Goulburn which came with the machinery needed to meet anticipated demand. Shortly after that he was contacted by a police superintendent who let it be known that a contribution of thirty thousand dollars would ensure Dunc's accreditation to produce the police equipment. 'I naturally refused his offer.' The unsurprising result – 'No police work'. It was both a bad career move and an accurate reflection of the state of the New South Wales police service at the time as the Wood Royal Commission subsequently revealed. With no police work coming in, the Goulburn factory had to be sold off. If that loss wasn't bad enough, the aftermath of the Port Arthur massacre was the final straw. John Howard's subsequent gun control legislation put a damper on the George Street businesses that Dunc had supplied for years. All of a sudden, 'firearm' was a dirty word and the demand for related leather goods slowly dried up. Undeterred, Dunc persisted with his work, although at a much-diminished rate.

To take his mind of his woes, Dunc went looking for something more personally gratifying. After the Mexico games he occupied himself with touch football and regular jogging, but the competitive urge remained as strong as ever. After he reached fifty, Pagey tried his hand at a form of weightlifting known as powerlifting. For most of his life, he had been interested in weight training. It began while jackarooing near Moree where he fashioned a set of barbells out of hollow tree trunks. By the age of fifty, he graduated to competing in master's powerlifting competitions.

Powerlifting was a thriving sport during the eighties and Dunc was right into it. In competitions the lifters amassed a cumulative total from three separate lifts – the squat, the deadlift and the bench press. Dunc thought that he might as well have a go. After performing successfully in several local Sydney competitions in the 82.5 kilo class, he stepped up and finished second in the Australian championships. Then it was off to Montreal in 1985 for the World Master's Games. Of course, there was a fly in the ointment. It was his bung leg – yes that again – and it severely limited his performance in the squat but had no effect on his deadlift or bench press. Dunc finished third in his class and admits that he 'learned a great deal by watching the techniques of the other competitors, most of whom were "on the juice"'. By 'juice' he is referring to anabolic steroids, the use of which was rampant in powerlifting circles as well as many other areas of athletic endeavour during that era.

Dunc watched carefully and learned well. He found that by adjusting his technique, his performances in the deadlift improved from 185 kilos to 240 kilos in a couple of months when he returned from Montreal. There were some who thought he could have done even better. Out of the blue one day, a fellow competitor arrived at his Bundeena house and sat down for a cup of tea. After a couple of sips, he informed Pagey that his performance would improve by twenty per cent if he started an anabolic steroid program. Dunc refused the offer 'flat out' even though the bloke who made it was an Australian placegetter in the world championships. Dunc was adamant that he intended to remain drug free. He then watched on in amazement when the Institute of Sport in Canberra offered to bankroll the sport of powerlifting on the condition that all states instituted a program of strict drug testing. It is instructive that when the AIS offer was tabled eighty per cent of competitors opted to join another powerlifting group 'where anything goes'. When the dust finally settled, two groups of lifters remained – those who were drug free and those who preferred open slather.

At the relatively advanced age of fifty plus – for an athlete – Dunc still wasn't interested in doing things by halves. Drug free he may have been, but that didn't hinder his determination to perform up to his maximum. All up Pagey won five Australian and numerous State powerlifting titles. In each win, his outstanding efforts in the deadlift and the bench press compensated for his leg-hindered results in the snatch. He considers the 1990 Australian Championship to be his ultimate performance. In that competition he defeated a former world champion who led him by 25 kilograms into the last lift – the deadlift. The pressure was on and it was a big ask but Dunc prevailed by 5 kilograms. You can do the maths to work out how much more he had to lift than his competitor to come home the winner. In all competitions the order of the lifts never varied; it was squat first, bench press second and finally the deadlift. Given that order, Pagey was always behind the eight ball. Far from stopping him, it was the impetus to improve in the other lifts. The handicap of his bad leg didn't stop him. Indeed, it was the motivation to set Australian records in the bench press and deadlift. Against drug-fuelled competitors in World Championships he came third and fourth. Performing in competitions where he always gave his utmost came at a cost. Despite learning to taper his training the week before a competition, the hundred per cent effort Dunc had to expend to win and set records often caused him to break out in cold sores afterward. He has no idea why and accepted that he had to put up with them as the cost of maximum effort. In powerlifting, as in everything else he did, Pagey never gave less than his all.

The lifting days ended as he got older and once again Dunc went looking for something to occupy himself. He needed to find something less strenuous. Something that didn't demand maximum physical effort. His mind went back to the days of his youth. The days with the trusty pistol – the one for which he traded away a mattress. He laughs as he recalls that the next firearm he bought was ordered by mail and how, in a more trusting age, 'It duly arrived by post and the postman left it on top of my letterbox'. Different times, indeed. The long and the short of these reminiscences was that Dunc began to compete in senior's pistol competitions. He didn't let himself down. In his seventies, Pagey was still capable of reeling off impressive scores that satisfied the most difficult of all people to please – Duncan McIntyre Page.

POSTSCRIPT

Today, if you take the drive through Royal National Park or catch the ferry from Cronulla you will eventually arrive at Bundeena. When you get there, keep a weather eye out for a sprightly elderly gentleman walking purposefully to the newsagent. Occasionally, if his leg is playing up, he may condescend to the use of a Zimmer frame. Whatever the weather or time of day, you will meet an invariably cheery and polite individual. The gentleman will cheerfully admit that to look at him now, there is no hint of the young athlete of half a century ago.

Dunc is well known to the locals, although very few know anything about his incredible sporting accomplishments. And why would they? The inherently modest man never utters a word. The only time he loosens up and recounts happy stories is when he is among the friends he has met along the way, especially Don and Pete, with whom he maintains regular contact. Pagey remains active and alert puttering around his Bundeena home. He is keenly interested in the things that have played a major part in his life – rugby league and thoroughbred horse racing. He is hardly the type of bloke to drift off into the fog of senility. He reads constantly, and the subjects are wide-ranging – with a leaning toward Australian sporting history. He is ever the welcoming host to those who come asking for reminiscences and to listen to him elaborate on his sporting history.

Despite the inevitable ups and downs of his life, Dunc remains content with his many and varied achievements. And so he should. There are few who can claim the length and breadth of the career he put together. Pagey is a living treasure and a walking library of an era of Australia's sporting history that can only be described as golden. The signal virtues he maintained from start to finish – honesty, maximum effort and an unquenchable desire to represent his country –are the measure of the man. He never gave less than his all, no matter what the endeavour. Dunc's example should stand as a shining beacon for coming generations.

Despite his lifelong love affair with thoroughbreds and the considerable sums he outlaid on his own horses, Pagey was never a punter. He candidly admits that he couldn't afford the risk. It took most of his ready cash just getting his horses to the racetrack. But there was more to not having a bet than chronic financial worries. Dunc knew enough about the thoroughbred 'industry' to leave the punt alone. 'I was well aware of all the shenanigans that went on behind the scenes, so very early on I decided it was best to keep my hands in my pockets.' That decision was nudged along by Bridget Woodford-Smith's tart observation about the racing game – 'Not all the people in racing are criminals, but all the criminals are in racing'. As for his devotion to racing, and against what many regarded as financial suicide, Dunc is adamant that he never considered it a burden. 'I loved every minute of it. You see, money to me has never meant a great deal. And racing gave me a great deal of satisfaction and was a great interest. I enjoyed it so much. For every thoroughbred there is a story – how they were bred, how they were trained, how they liked to race – it was a lifelong fixation.' That's all well and good but, given half a chance, Duncan would still love to breed the next Melbourne Cup winner.

Not long ago, over a cup of tea in his Bundeena home, I asked Dunc if there was anything more he would like to add to his recollections, anything he wanted on the record. He put his cup down gently and said in a voice laden with regret. 'I wish I had told my dad that, in my eyes, he was the best father a man could have had. He was very caring of Mum and just a good fella. But I never got around to telling him. I regret that.'

'I also wish I had never broken my leg. If I hadn't broken it, who knows what I might have been able to do? Ah well, I did the best I could. Once the leg was broken, there was nothing I could do about it. In pentathlon, I always felt I had no chance of winning. I was stymied by the bad leg. At the last event (always the run) I knew I had no show.'

The conversation continued and only ended when, in a voice of contentment, he said, 'I've had a good life'. He went quiet for a moment and again, repeating himself as if for emphasis, Dunc said, 'I've had a good life'.

ABOUT THE AUTHOR

Hunter Calder and Duncan Page have been great mates for the better part of fifty years. The events in this book were slowly revealed during that time. During their many travels together, Hunter regularly promised that 'one day' they would be chronicled. That day came during the coronavirus period when *Unstoppable* – the promise from one mate to another – became a reality. At long last, the remarkable events of Duncan Page's life have been given the light of day.

Hunter Calder is the International Literacy Year award-winning author and co-founder of the online literacy program 'Literacy Planet'. He currently lives on the south coast of NSW with his wife, Lorna, where he and his wife Lorna watch their children make their marks in the world.

www.ingramcontent.com/pod-product-compliance
Lightning Source LLC
Chambersburg PA
CBHW051357290426
44108CB00015B/2051